G000089620

Roger P. Booth
B.D., Ph.D., LL.B., A.K.C.

DOWN TO EARTH

Thoughts of a Free Christian

AUSTIN MACAULEY PUBLISHERS™

LONDON • CAMBRIDGE • NEW YORK • SHARJAH

Copyright © Roger P. Booth (2019)

The right of Roger P. Booth to be identified as author of this work has been asserted by him in accordance with section 77 and 78 of the Copyright, Designs and Patents Act 1988.

All rights reserved. No part of this publication may be reproduced, stored in a retrieval system, or transmitted in any form or by any means, electronic, mechanical, photocopying, recording, or otherwise, without the prior permission of the publishers.

Any person who commits any unauthorised act in relation to this publication may be liable to criminal prosecution and civil claims for damages.

A CIP catalogue record for this title is available from the British Library.

ISBN 9781528901383 (Paperback)
ISBN 9781528957243 (ePub e-book)

www.austinmacauley.com

First Published (2019)
Austin Macauley Publishers Ltd
25 Canada Square
Canary Wharf
London
E14 5LQ

This book is dedicated to my great friend, Allan Preston.

Acknowledgement

The author wishes to acknowledge that the book contains
writing which originally appeared in *The Christian
Compass* and *The Liberal Christian Herald*.

Table of Contents

Foreword

In this book I have in part collected together some articles and sermons which I have revised for publication. The impetus to publish was my concern that potential followers of Jesus might be deterred from serving him by the supernatural elements in the orthodox beliefs about him. I have accordingly studied the influence of the supernatural and other alleged ways of communication by God. I use the word 'supernatural' to denote any happening which conflicts with the laws of nature (e.g. chemistry, physics and biology).

The essential belief which undermines my thinking about theology is in the fact that God created the universe. This belief is based on the dictum of Descartes, 'cogito ergo sum' (I think, therefore I am). Because I thus exist a power must have created me and the rest of the universe. Consequently, nothing is impossible for the creator of everything from planets to microbes. We cannot deny any claim by a miraculous being possessing such limitless powers. To turn water into wine or to walk on water are but the trivia of the supernatural to such a power. Similarly, it was the power of God which enabled Jesus to effect the cures related in the Gospels. (Luke 5:17 – "the power of the Lord was upon him"; Acts 2:22 "which God did by him"). Only the surrounding circumstances may convince me that an alleged act contrary to the laws of nature is in fact not authentic. The question is not—"Did God have power to cause a virginal conception or the assumption of human form?" but "Does the context render the divine actions likely?"

God's creation of the universe carries the corollary that all human achievements, whatever they may be, are the result of God-given powers.

This liberal Christian approach to Jesus's life and death then prompted me to examine several Gospel incidents and teachings which were probably elaborated by followers who wished to magnify the mystery and glory surrounding him.

Thinking on these liberal lines induced me to discuss firstly, a liberal approach to the principal beliefs about Jesus, secondly, the theological reasoning underpinning those beliefs, and lastly, some aspects of the Jewish laws which impinged on those beliefs. This led to consideration of the extent to which followers of Jesus—to whom the Jewish laws and traditions were a natural inheritance—are themselves bound by them.

It is important to note the vulnerability to corruption which the texts of the Hebrew scriptures and the Gospels suffer. The vowel signs in the words of the former were not settled until the Masorete rabbis fixed them in the 6th to 7th centuries B.C.E. These signs were placed below, above or between the trilateral consonants, and the meaning of a verb might be radically altered by the reader's choice of vowel. Thus at Song of Songs 5:16, a Hebrew word is translated as 'altogether lovely'. Before written vowels were introduced, only the consonants were written (as in the synagogue scriptures today). The consonants at 5:16, D M H M, could be supplied with vowels which would create the word 'MAHUM(M)AD'. Some Muslim critics have considered this to be a reference in the scriptures to Muhammad. Jesus spoke the Aramaic tongue and several factors may have caused a discrepancy between the meaning which Jesus intended and the version reported in the Gospels. His audience may have mis-heard his speech or those first hearers or subsequent tradents may have unintentionally altered the story to some degree by embellishment or omission. Also, in the passing on of the story to a Greek speaker nuances of meaning may have been lost due to cultural differences in the Jewish and Gentile backgrounds. The further translation into English may have involved slight changes of meaning since translation is not an exact science.

That changes did in fact occur in the transmission of the sayings of Jesus is shown by the reports of particular sayings and deeds in the different Gospels. Thus at Mark 11:11–12 Jesus declares that any divorcee who marries again, commits

9

adultery, whereas in Matthew's source (5:32) the divorcee who divorces on the ground of unchastity is excepted from this ruling. It is therefore wise not to place great emphasis on any particular saying or act of Jesus but rather to rely on its consistency or inconsistency of meaning with other sayings or acts on the same general subject.

It is mistaken to view every word in the Gospels as inspired by God for there are some obvious inaccuracies. For example, the attribution to Isaiah of the whole of the quotation in Mark 1:2–3 is incorrect since verse 2 is a variation of the Septuagint version of Malachi 3:1, not Isaiah. This is of little importance in itself but it does prejudice the argument supporting the verbal inspiration of the Gospels.

The same reservation must be made regarding the Hebrew scriptures. Thus the English translation of the words in Isaiah 7:14 is—"the young woman is with child and will bear a son". The Hebrew words—'ha almah' meaning 'young woman' without reference to virginity were translated in the LXX (the official translation of the Hebrew scriptures into Greek) by the Greek 'he parthenos' which means a virgin. This mistranslation has supported the fundamental belief at the core of Christianity that Mary the mother of Jesus was a virgin.

Again, there is a potential mistranslation of the Aramaic 'de' probably used by Jesus at Mark 4:11 where he enigmatically states that everything comes in parables to those outside the kingdom in order that they may look but not perceive... so that they may not turn again and be forgiven. This is a difficult saying because the purpose of Jesus' ministry was to bring people to repentance and forgiveness, not turn them away. The cause of this difficulty may lie in this use of the Aramaic particle 'de' which can mean either 'in order that' (a relative clause) or 'who' (a descriptive clause). If it is translated as 'who' then the teaching more consistently is that everything comes in parables to those outside who look but do not perceive, for if they did perceive they would be forgiven.

In a book which focuses on beliefs and reasoning a caveat should be recorded against the danger of over-estimating the importance of particular beliefs (e.g. on the incarnation) in the spiritual life of the Christian. For in times of such emotional stress they are unlikely to be uppermost in their minds. The depth of assurance of the presence of God is likely to dominate. Consciousness of God, not intellectual positions will probably be the controlling thought.

Finally, in any study of the life of Jesus the influence of Rome must be noted. The subjugation of their God-given land to Roman imperium was a seething humiliation to the Jews, and the desire to rid themselves of this offence to Yahweh was uppermost in the minds of Jesus' contemporaries. Although limited powers were given to the Jewish Sanhedrin, Josephus records that after the death of Herod the Great in 4BCE. Judea was filled with insurrection. Gamaliel reminds the Sanhedrin of the revolts of Theudas and Judas the Galilean (Acts 5,36-37). Jerusalem was sacked by the Romans in C.E.66.

Chapter 1
The Principal Beliefs About Jesus

It is appropriate, at the outset, to consider the most prominent features of liberal Christianity. Probably many would-be followers of Jesus are deterred by the orthodox understanding of him as a member of the Trinity i.e., as God. Yet it is arguable that he was a human being who was extremely close to God, and through whom God revealed his will as to how human beings should live. This assessment of his status avoids the need to accept the supernatural elements of the Christian creed such as the virgin birth, the atonement and a physical bodily resurrection. On this basis, a summary of his life would be on the following lines:

1. At his baptism God called Jesus 'Son of God' (Mark 1:11). This was a name given to a person who was anointed (appointed) by God for a particular task. In Jesus' case, the task was to bring in the Kingdom. The words 'Christ' and 'Messiah' also meant 'anointed' and were understood to refer to the 'prophet like Moses' whom God would raise up and into whose mouth God would put his words (Deuteronomy 18:15–18; Mark 9:7).

2. This appointed task commenced when Jesus preached the good news of God after John the Baptist was arrested. The news was that the time was fulfilled, the Kingdom of God was at hand, and people should repent and believe in the good news (Mark 1:14–15). He publicised his belief that he was the Christ when in the synagogue at Nazareth he read Isaiah's words that the Lord had anointed him (Isaiah) to bring good news to the poor, release to the captives, give sight to

the blind and freedom to the oppressed. For he then said, "Today this scripture has been fulfilled in your hearing." (Luke 4: 16–21).

3. He implicitly expressed his belief in himself as the prophet 'who is to come'. When John's disciples asked whether he was that person or whether they should look for another he replied, "Go and tell John that the blind receive their sight, the lame walk, the deaf hear and the poor have good news preached to them." (Luke 7:18–22).

4. So Jesus preached, cast out demons and healed but was rejected by the people. He exclaimed, "Woe to you, Chorazin! Woe to you, Bethsaida! For if the mighty work that has been done to you, had been done to Tyre and Sidon, they would have repented long ago, sitting in sackcloth and ashes." (Mathew 11:21).

5. When Peter identified Jesus as Christ, Jesus told him that he (Jesus) would be rejected by the elders and the chief priests, and would be killed and rise again in three days (Mark 8:31).

6. Thus Jesus implied that he, indeed, was the Christ but not the war-like 'Son of David' type of Christ. He was the 'suffering servant' type of Christ described in Isaiah (53) who would "bear the sin of many and make intercession for the transgressors" (v .12).

7. Jesus believed that because the people did not repent, God would delay the introduction of the Kingdom (Luke 13:34–35), and he, therefore, decided that he, Jesus, would have to suffer in substitution for the people as a ransom for their sins (Mark 10:45). Through his suffering, Jesus would make the ransom 'payment' to release the people from their suffering which was due on account of their sins.

8. Furthermore, he believed that his death would constitute the sacrifice that could be offered to make the 'new covenant' between God and His people. This covenant was promised in Jeremiah (31:34) and pursuant to it the people would know God directly for He would forgive their sins. His blood would solemnize this new covenant. Thus at the last supper,

13

he said that his body would be broken like the bread and his blood poured out like the wine–as the blood of the new covenant (Mark 14:24; Luke 22:20).

9. It appears that Jesus was mistaken in thinking that God would then bring in the Kingdom, since sin is still rampant in the world. However, it may be thought that the principles of the Kingdom will gradually overcome the world. As the leaven imperceptivity changes the dough and the seed sprouts, it is argued that the behaviour of the followers of Jesus may increase the influence of the Kingdom (Luke 13:20–21; Mark 4:26–28).

10. It is also argued that Jesus was mistaken in thinking that his Father wanted him to die as a ransom for the sins of the people since a loving God would not want anyone to die for the sins of another. However, Jesus may have had this concept about his death because substitutional suffering was a recognised element in Jewish thinking. Thus a ram was offered for sacrifice in substitution for the killing of Isaac (Genesis 22:13) and in 4 Maccabees Eleazar asks God to take his life as a ransom for the lives of the people (6:29). In Temple ritual the sacrifice of animals was substituted for the punishment of the people for their sins.

11. Jesus died in great anguish, "My God, why have you forsaken me?" (Mark 15:34). The great benefit conferred by his death was that he showed by example that his followers should obey God's will even if it involved the supreme sacrifice.

12. He prayed, "Abba, Father, all things are possible to thee; remove this cup from me; yet not what I wilt but what thou wilt." (Mark 14:36). The supreme function achieved by Jesus' life was that in his teaching and healing God revealed to mankind how they should live.

13. Jesus expected that after his ascension he would return as the 'Son of Man', "coming with the clouds of heaven" (Mark 14:62; Daniel 7:13) to inaugurate the Kingdom of God. He has not yet so returned.

Chapter 2
God's Communication with Man

"No one has ever seen God; it is the only Son, who is in the bosom of the Father, who has made him known."– John (1:18).

The fact that no one has seen God does not prove that God does not exist. A Russian astronaut and an atheist were discussing religion with a Russian brain-surgeon who was a Christian. The astronaut said, "I've made several trips into space, but I've never seen God or his angels". The brain surgeon replied, "Well, I've operated on the brains of many clever people, but I've never seen any thoughts." The point of the story is that thoughts can exist even though they're invisible, so why shouldn't God exist even though we can't see him.

Even though we can't see thoughts, we can prove that they exist because our bodies couldn't function without them. My arm would not lift this paper unless a thought of the wish to lift it passed from my brain to my arm. Our emotions are thoughts and they also affect our bodily activities. Fear can cause us to shiver and anxiety can affect our stomach. It's remarkable that not only can our intangible thoughts influence our bodies in this way but that those thoughts are presumably produced by the tangible cells from our brain.

Or are they so produced?

Professor David Fontana, ex-President of the Society for Psychical Research recently wrote that we are no nearer to establishing how the electrochemical activity of a material brain can cause non-physical activity like thoughts. And we are no nearer to discovering exactly where in the brain, consciousness (the knowledge that we're alive) is produced.

There are arguments for maintaining that mental events operate *through* the brain rather than arise *from* it.

Mystical, psychic, out-of-body and near-death experiences all point to the existence of a non-physical mind that can operate outside the brain and that survives its death.

God, too, is invisible like our thoughts. The example of our thoughts shows that God could exist even though invisible, and we doubt at our peril that electricity and gas exist though invisible. Reasoning can prove that thoughts exist but cannot satisfactorily prove that God exists.

Descartes, the great 17th century rationalist philosopher, did attempt to prove God's existence by the nature of our thoughts. God must exist, he argued, "Because I can think of a perfect being that I call God. And that perfect being wouldn't be perfect if it didn't exist—therefore, that perfect being, God, must exist." But there seems to be a non sequitur here in the linking of the quality of perfection with the condition of existence.

The strongest evidence for the existence of God is the created universe which as Aristotle and Aquinas claimed, must have been formed by a 'first mover'. This evidence is countered by the doubt over a self-created 'first mover'.

Which is more likely—a self-created 'first mover' or a self-created universe? The achievement of reason may be considered limited—it is only shown to be not unreasonable to believe in a creator, God, despite His invisibility.

In any case, many believers in God do not need rational proof of His existence since they have received direct communication from Him. Among those privileged thus stand the prophets of Israel, Jesus Christ, Muhammad, Joseph Smith and mystics throughout the ages. They believe God exists because they believe He has spoken to them.

But for those of us who have not experienced direct communication from God, the experiences of others are evidence but not proof of his existence. Religious experiences can be illusory and unless we have personally experienced God's voice speaking to us there may be doubt in our minds as to whether others have been deceived. For people have been deceived and divine authority has been claimed for wicked and deranged deeds. We wish that the evidence of those who claim to have received divine communication could

16

be corroborated but that confirmation could only be from the person who communicated with God himself. So the rest of us have to proceed with that faith (Greek, pistis) described at Hebrews 11:1 as "the assurance of things hoped for, the conviction of things not seen."

The things hoped for and not seen surely include God's existence and His support of us on the journey of life. That faith is strengthened by Jesus, who was visible in flesh and blood in the first century and was able by his own words and deeds, to reveal God's will to us all.

How does God communicate with people?

Many people of faith claim that God has communicated with them during prayer or otherwise. Some believe that God has spoken to them through the voice of conscience. Such fortunate people do not need to analyse the evidence for their claim because they have experienced the communication personally. But for people without that personal experience, the question of whether God has communicated with other people can only be answered from a rationalist standpoint through weighing the evidence supporting and opposing the claim. For the principal counter-evidence against a divine communication consists of the amazing nature of the claim. Indeed, the evidence against such a communication appears so strong that the validity of the claim must depend on the compelling nature of any corroboration produced to support it. The strongest corroboration would be a confirmatory message from God, but that would be extremely unlikely. However, corroboration could be provided by another person or persons who could testify that the alleged communication from God was made in their hearing also.

There are many assertions by writers in the Old Testament that God has communicated with people on earth. Exodus 3 and 4 are full of alleged conversation between God and Moses. God also spoke to the prophets, e.g., to Samuel at 1 Samuel 3:4–14; to Elijah at 1 Kings 19:9. He also spoke to Solomon at 1 Kings 3:10–14. Yet the assembly at Horeb believed that if they heard the voice of God, they would die (Deuteronomy 5:15; 18:16).

There are also assertions of God-like communications in the New Testament. It is reported that after his baptism Jesus saw the heavens open and the Spirit descending like a dove and he heard a voice from heaven, "Thou art my beloved son; with thee I am well pleased" (Mark 1:11).

This is a vision but God may speak through visions and dreams. At Mark (9:2–8), Peter, James and John see Jesus transfigured with Moses and Elijah, and hear a voice from the cloud, "This is my beloved Son; listen to him". This again is a vision but the words of God are presumably witnessed by the three disciples.

In Acts (10:10–16), Peter, in a trance, saw a great sheet with all kinds of animals on it, and heard a voice from heaven commanding him to kill and eat. Peter demurs but the voice says, "What God has cleansed you must not call common." This happened three times. God here condemned Peter's natural Jewish inclination to abstain from ritually unclean food. This inclination appears subsequently in his eating separately from Gentiles (Galatians 2:12).

At his conversion in Acts (9:3–8), Paul and the spirit of the risen Jesus speak together and Jesus commands Paul to enter Damascus and receive further instructions. A light from heaven flashes about Paul and this also indicates a vision.

Paul indicates in 2 Corinthians (12:1–4), that he had other contacts with the spirit world. In verses 8–9, he describes how three times he asked Jesus for relief from his 'thorn in the flesh' and received the reply, "My grace is sufficient for you, for my power is made perfect in weakness." Paul is unlikely to have invented this reply since he presumably wanted to hear that the 'thorn' would be removed.

The Holy Spirit may be understood as the voice of God. In Acts 16:6 Paul and Silas are forbidden by the Holy Spirit to speak the word in Asia. In verse 7, the Spirit prevents them from going into Bithynia. Presumably, the Spirit here is answering their requests for guidance.

Naturally, there is no corroboration by God or Jesus that they have made these communications so a decision on whether they did communicate in these and other instances has to be based upon a review of the evidence supporting and opposing the communication. Evidence against the assertion of words from God consists, as mentioned above, in the enormity of the claim that the Creator Spirit has spoken to people on earth. However, for those enquirers who accept the possibility of speech from the spirit of a deceased person with a person on earth, the force of this unlikelihood is weakened.

For if there is testimony that other spirits have communicated with people on earth, how much more likely is it that God, being the almighty Creator Spirit, and the spirit of Jesus, may also have communicated. There would thus be evidence that there are open 'pathways' from heaven to earth which have been trodden by some spirits and may also have been traversed by the Creator Spirit and the spirit of the risen Jesus.

The resurrection of Jesus and the existence of spirits of the deceased are basic tenets of the Christian faith, for the risen Jesus was "the first fruits of those who have died." (1 Corinthians, 15:20).

In the Synoptic Gospels Jesus has not said that the spirits of the dead can communicate with earth but an implication to that effect might be drawn from the Transfiguration where the risen Moses and Elijah speak to the earthly Jesus in the presence of the disciples (Mark 9:4).

A Biblical assertion of a non-divine spirit communicating to earth is made at 1 Samuel 28 where the deceased Samuel appears to Saul and converses with him.

Modern alleged instances of communication by spirits of deceased humans have been collected by the Society for Psychical Research. David Fontana examined closely the circumstances and content of communications made by many spirits who have allegedly communicated through various mediums– particularly through Leonora Piper, Gladys Leonard and Eileen Garrett. He concluded that, "if you believe that you are more than a biological accident whose ultimately meaningless life is bounded by the cradle and the grave, I agree with you." (l)

If the assertion of such communications were supported by substantiating evidence, then the proven ability of these non-divine spirits to communicate with people on earth would increase the possibility of communications by God, the Creator Spirit. The necessary corroboration of such communications by these non-divine spirits may consist of any circumstance which renders the authenticity of the communication alleged more probable. Thus as mentioned above, voices heard by more than one person at a time may be such a circumstance (e.g. many people were present at the time of the visions of, and conversation with, the Virgin Mary at Medjugorje Yugoslavia).

The book and newspaper tests provided for the Reverend Drayton Thomas (2) and the 'spirit' photograph of himself provided by the spirit of Conan Doyle (3) seem to be other examples of satisfactory corroboration of the communications alleged. It is arguable that the tapes allegedly recording spirit voices (such as those of Elizabeth Fry, Father O'Leary and Ted Butler) in conversation with living people are persuasive corroboration of their communications. No absolute proof of the genuineness of these communications can be adduced, but there are so many recorded instances where communication by the spirit of a deceased may be thought to be satisfactorily corroborated that the cumulative weight of their evidence strongly supports the possibility of communication by God to people on earth.

However, counter-evidence set against the alleged communication by God may consist not only in the amazing fact of God so communicating, but also in any inconsistency between the content of the communication and the virtues of God (see pp. 25-26).

Communication by Vision and Conscience

Isaiah (1 and 6) and Ezekiel (1) received the subject of prophecies in vision. They caused the prophecies to be written down for various reasons – preservation and in Jeremiah's case to reach the Temple from which he was barred. Three times Samuel hears a voice calling him and he thinks it is Eli. The third time Eli tells Samuel to say, "Speak. Lord, for thy servant heareth." God then gives Samuel an important message for Eli (1 Samuel 3). The word of the Lord was rare in those days, which implies that in previous days, there had been frequent communications from God.

It appears that God often speaks to people in dreams at night. The angel of the Lord appeared three times to Joseph, the husband of Mary, while he dreamt. God appears to others in a vision while they are awake or during the daytime. The prophet Ezekiel wrote, "as I was among the exiles by the river Chebar, the heavens were opened and I saw visions of God.' (1:1)

But the most documented communication from the heavens was the appearance of Jesus to Saul (or Paul as we know him better), on the road to Damascus. Luke, who wrote the Acts of the Apostles, has Paul describing his experience not only in chapter 9 but also in chapter 22 before the Roman tribune in Jerusalem, and in chapter 26 before King Agrippa in Caesarea. Paul himself refers to Jesus' appearance to him, "Last of all as to one untimely born he appeared also to me" (1 Corinthians 15:3). Most of what Paul writes in his letters is very good evidence because it is not second-hand, it is Paul himself speaking.

Clearly some persons are spiritually sensitive and privileged to receive direct communication from God or the spirit of Jesus or from the spirits of their departed loved ones. Thus Paul writes, "I know a man in Christ who, 14 years ago, was caught up to the third heaven—caught up into Paradise whether in body or out of body—I know not." (2 Corinthians 12). Paul is thought here to be referring obliquely to himself. Samuel, perhaps due to his youth, did not realise that it was God who was speaking to him.

We need to be able to distinguish the true communications from God from the inauthentic since we know what dastardly things have been committed by dictators and others believing that they have been authorised by their God. Jesus said to those claiming to be prophets, "By their fruits you shall know them" (Matthew 7:20) and if we should wonder whether a communicated course of action is from God, a reliable criterion is whether the action will benefit others rather than ourselves.

Perhaps the most frequent way in which God may speak to us is through our conscience.

In discussing the standard of conduct expected of a Christian R.C Mortimer wrote, "The first rule is to obey conscience; where conscience gives a clear ruling, deliberately and knowingly to disobey; it is sinful. The concept of sin plays a large part in Christian ethics. Its form and essence is deliberate disobedience to God. It is the work of conscience to

21

tell a man on every occasion what is the will of God. Hence, to disobey conscience is to disobey God. It often happens, of course, that what a man's conscience tells him to do is not in fact God's will. Yet even so to disobey conscience is to disobey God for the man refuses to do what he thinks is God's will."

To act repeatedly against the call of conscience is habit-forming like any other repeated act, and that dulls the conscience and makes it less sensitive to sometimes fine distinctions between right and wrong. But prayer and Bible-reading will help to keep the conscience tender. Our conscience may warn us not to do some wrongful act, or urge us to do something which for selfish reasons we do not want to do. And our consciences may afflict us with remorse when we fail to follow its dictates. Paul's conscience probably covered him with remorse and guilt for his persecution of Jesus since his conscience urged him to follow Jesus. But fighting against his conscience was perhaps his unwillingness to accept the lifestyle change from the rôle of respected Pharisaic leader to that of follower of a small Jewish sect. Perhaps the crisis of conscience provoked the vision, for Jesus asks him in the vision, "Saul, Saul, why do you persecute me? It is hard for you this kicking against the goads." However, the goads of Paul's conscience prevail and Paul is converted to the Way, and becomes foremost in bringing knowledge of Jesus to the Gentiles.

Communication by Dreams

Isaac and Rebekah didn't want Jacob to marry one of the local Canaanite girls, so they sent him off to Padan Aram in the North to marry one of their own tribe, a daughter of Laban, Rebekah's brother. So Jacob left Beer-Sheba in Canaan and when the sun had set, he stopped for the night. He was sleeping in the open for he had a stone for a pillow.

And he had a dream. He dreamt that there was a ladder set up on the earth, the top of it reached to heaven and the angels of God were ascending and descending on it. And God stood above it and promised to give the land on which he lay to him and his descendants. That land was Canaan for Jacob had not travelled far from Beer-Sheba as yet. God's promise was fulfilled when after the Exodus from Egypt and the wandering in the wilderness, Moses led the Israelites to the Promised Land of Canaan. "Behold, I am with you and will keep you wherever you go, and will bring you back to this land; for I will not leave you until I have done what I have promised you," (Genesis 28:15). God often communicates with men and women in dreams in the Biblical stories. In the nativity story in Matthew, an angel tells Joseph to take Mary as his wife for she has conceived by the Holy Spirit, and again he is warned by an angel to flee with Mary and the baby to Egypt to avoid Herod's wrath. The message of those dreams was clear, but often dreams need interpreting. Thus an earlier Joseph gained favour by interpreting the dreams of Pharaoh.

So how is this dream of Jacob to be interpreted? Sigmund Freud claimed that dreams had a manifest or obvious content and a latent or hidden content. The manifest content of Jacob's dream is of the angel's descending and ascending on the ladder. The hidden content or meaning may be that God was telling Jacob through the dream that he, God, was concerned and interested in Jacob's earthly endeavours. Jacob could communicate with God in prayer, which would rise to God like an angel ascending the ladder. God would in turn communicate with Jacob by engendering dreams which would reach Jacob like an angel descending the ladder from heaven.

Certainly, when Jacob awoke, he realised that God was present to him there. He said, "Surely the Lord is in this place; and I did not know it. How awesome is this place!" (Genesis 28: 16-17)

Our sins are not a barrier to the ascent of that ladder .For Jacob had not led a blameless life. Jacob forced Esau, who was about to die of hunger, to sell him his birth right, his entitlement to his inheritance, simply in exchange for the food, the mess of pottage that Jacob was brewing. Also, Jacob colluded with his mother to obtain his father's blessing by dressing himself in goat skins so that his blind father, Isaac, would think he was Esau, and give him the blessing. But despite these grave wrongs to his brother, God gave a wonderful revelation to Jacob in his dream. So following Jesus teaching, if we forgive others, God will forgive us, and our prayers will climb the ladder.

Communication through Prayer

Does prayer have any effect?

Many people of faith will answer with a resounding 'yes' to such a question because they have experienced the effects of prayer in their own lives. However, the question deserves discussion from the standpoint of reason. Religious prayer presumes a channel of communication between God and man, and is central to the practice of religion. Belief in the existence of a God is therefore necessary, and prayer may be defined as talk with God. In much talk with God, the making of petitions to God is an important element. If the petitions were to be shown to have been answered, the effectiveness of prayer and the existence of God would both be proved. Human beings have an instinct to seek the help of a deity when confronted by problems. The request to the deity for help may be communicated by sacrifice or dance or prayer. It may seek rain for a good harvest or human fertility or relief in any other need. We must consider first whether a channel of communication between human beings and a supernatural God is possible. Morse code and radio have shown that messages can be sent from human to human over distance without the use of the eyes or the need for physical presence. Tests carried out by J.B. Rhines and others have shown that thoughts can be transferred between humans by telepathy, i.e. by the power of the minds of the transmitter and the recipient. It seems possible that thought in the form of prayer can be transferred to God in a similar way.

Moreover, just as the transfer of sound by airwaves was thought impossible until the discovery of radio, so the transfer of thought to God may be discovered in the future to be a process consistent with the laws of physics.

Assuming that this transfer of thought to God in prayer is possible, how can the petitioner know whether the deity has been moved to action by the request?

If God is all-powerful, he is able to grant the prayer. But there is evidence that his powers are limited by the natural laws which he established at creation, namely the laws of chemistry, physics and biology. For God is described in the Bible as loving and merciful, yet he does not intervene to over-reach the physical laws which produce the natural evils

24

afflicting mankind. For example, he does not prevent cells from coalescing and becoming cancerous nor does he prevent the fracturing of the earth's crust which causes an earthquake. Admittedly, to counteract such happenings would necessitate gigantic interference with the operation of the laws established at creation, but a risk-free environment would not be beyond the power of an omnipotent God. And being a loving God, he must desire to prevent these evils.

Therefore, the fact that they occur must be due to his inability to curtail the operations of the natural laws which cause them.

However, there are situations in which the grant of the prayer would not necessitate a breach of the natural laws. For example, a request that God will grant peace of mind would not involve such a breach. Turning distress of mind to peace would involve influencing the thought process of the sufferer, but that does not involve a breach of the biological laws, since the thought processes of human beings are always influenced by the speech and actions of other humans in accordance with the natural working of the brain. But even in these cases the prayer may not effect or change anything, because, being omniscient, God is aware of all instances of suffering and as a loving God he has already taken appropriate actions regarding them, irrespective of the prayers received.

Prayer may, however, have effect in the following ways. Human beings have, as mentioned, an instinctive urge to plead to the deity for protection in times of trouble and the appeal to a supernatural power may give cathartic relief to the petitioner. Secondly, where the patient knows (by word of mouth or by telepathy or other means) that people have been asking God for the patient's recovery or other welfare, this may encourage the patient's state of mind which may psychosomatically aid the recovery of the patient's body. Thirdly, prayer by a patient for healing may be effective if accompanied by faith that the prayer will be answered. Jesus said to a woman with an issue of blood whom he cured, "Your faith (meaning trust or belief) has made you well." (Mark 5:34). For the patient's prayer may manifest such trust in God's willingness to heal that this trusting state of mind may, again psychosomatically, effect a bodily cure. However, the content of the alleged communication may be incompatible with the qualities of God revealed in scripture. Thus the reported words of God at 1 Samuel (15:3) that Saul should smite every man, woman and child of Amalek conflict with the Biblical description of a God of mercy. Again, God's alleged assertion (a 'bath qol') in a rabbinic dispute that the opinion of Rabbi Eliezer was always correct, is faced with the counter-evidence of the unlikelihood of God making and announcing a judgment of this nature (Bab.M.59b).

We accordingly conclude that, even in the absence of personal experience, it is possible to believe that God does communicate with people. But whether God has in a particular instance communicated with a person on earth should be judged on whether the balance of evidence, assessed in accordance with the above considerations, renders the communication more probable than not. And the decision there has potentially another important consequence for if God does communicate with people then, ipso facto, his existence becomes incontrovertible.

Notes:

(1) David Fontana, Is there an afterlife? (0-Books, 2005).
(2) Drayton Thomas, C. Life beyond Death with Evidence. (Collins, 1928)
(3) Cooke, I, The Return Of Arthur Conan Doyle (White Eagle publishing trust, 1963)

"For my thoughts are not your thoughts, neither are your ways my ways, says the Lord," (Isaiah 55:8).

These words were spoken by the second Isaiah to the exiled Jews in Babylon. He had told them how God would raise up Cyrus, King of the Medes, who would conquer Babylon and allow the exiles to return to Jerusalem and Judea. But many of them were preoccupied with their interests in Babylon and distrustful of Isaiah's prophecies of what God would do for them, through Cyrus. So Isaiah is here explaining that they should not worry since God is not obstructed by what appear as difficulties to mortal men, "For as the heavens are higher than the earth, so are my ways higher than your ways and my thoughts than your thoughts" (55:9).

An aspect of the philosophy of Immanuel Kant supports this limitation on human powers of thought. He was born in 1724 in the East Prussian town of Konigsberg, and lived there nearly all his life till his death at 80. He was the first great philosopher to be a University teacher. Punctual in his habits, people checked the time by his afternoon walk. Up to his time philosophers had been either rationalists or empiricists. The empiricists believed you could only know about the world what your senses, i.e. eyes, ears, nose and touch, told you. The rationalists believed the senses could deceive, e.g. optical illusions, dreams, and that you could only be sure of knowing what reasoning and logic showed to be true.

Immanuel Kant supported both views to a limited extent. With some exceptions, he argued, we can accept as authentic what we perceive through our senses (eyesight, hearing, etc.) but our brains are programmed to process this information in a particular way.

For everything has to fit our in-built requirements of time, space and causation. Our human brains are conditioned to mould what we see or hear into certain patterns. Just as water poured into a jug takes the shape of the jug, so everything we experience with our senses has to conform to our brain patterns of time, space and causation. So, what we experience may be a different thing from the thing in itself, the *Ding an sich*. If we wear spectacles with green-coloured lenses then everything looks green to us. Equally, everything we see with human eyes we analyse according to our human conceptions.

It seems likely that these brain parameters were created by habit rather than born with us.

If a ball of wool is thrown into a room, a baby will probably crawl after it, whereas, an adult will look to see who threw it. Adults have observed for so long that nothing happens without something else causing it, that they are programmed by habit to expect causation whenever anything moves. In contrast, the baby's mind, a 'tabula rasa', has not been habituated. Similarly, adults expect something to have a commencement in time and to extend in space.

Aristotle of the 4th century BC and Aquinas of the 13th century CE, both used the argument of causation to prove the existence of God. Nothing changes or moves unless something else causes it to do so. My book is not raised to my eyes unless my hand lifts it. The earth does not warm up unless the sun heats it. But in the beginning, they argued, there must have been a first mover to set the world going, and that first mover we call God.

But the question then arising about that creator God is, "Who made Him?" The usual answer is that God is self-created or has existed eternally, forever. Yet we have difficulty with this solution. Our human mind-set, programmed with the dogma of causation, almost forbids the possibility that something created itself—was an unmoved mover—and our mental dogma of time doubts whether anything could exist without having had a beginning.

Yet it's surely right for us to grapple with such problems: God gave us brains to be used. Jesus challenged his disciples to think for themselves, 'Who do men say that I am? But who do you say that I am?" (Mark 8:27–29). Yet when we come to think about God, perhaps we have to acknowledge the insight of Immanuel Kant that our human minds have become programmed to understand things according to earthly habits of thought. Those habits of thought may prevent us from seeing some things, particularly heavenly things, as they really are, for 'as the heavens are higher than the earth, so are my ways higher than your ways and my thoughts than your thoughts.'

Thus Mark reports that some people thought that the living Jesus was John the Baptist, resurrected with his human body (8:28), as did Herod (6:16). This belief is opposed by the fact that corpses disintegrate. It would, however, explain the origin of the stories that Jesus ate food and showed his hands and feet. Since to convince the Jews of Jesus' resurrection, it would be necessary to show that he retained his human body.

Alternatively, the Gospel assertions about Jesus' appearances could be interpreted as meaning that they were subjective, internal experiences of the disciples. The psychiatric term for 'seeing' something which has no reality outside the 'seer' is an hallucination. An hallucination may be caused by severe tension and the disciples would suffer from stress on the death of Jesus and the expectation of his immediate return. However, hallucinations by more than one person (collective hallucinations) are rare and the considerable amount of speech and activity of Jesus during the appearances renders this an unlikely explanation.

The evidence of Jesus appearing with a spiritual, immaterial, body seems more cogent. He appears suddenly and vanishes both on the road to Emmaus and in Jerusalem and rises into a cloud at Bethany. Paul stresses that there are both heavenly and earthly bodies, "It is sown a physical body, it is raised a spiritual body" (1 Corinthians 15:44). Consistent with this is Jesus' reply to a questioner that there were no marriages in the after-life for they are like "angels in heaven" (Mark 12:25).

Only about 20 years after the crucifixion, Paul wrote that he had passed on to the disciples what he had received, namely that Jesus appeared to Peter and the disciples.

His assertion that Jesus also appeared in front of more than 500 people at the same time seems exaggerated, even though collective visions of the Virgin Mary are reported to have been experienced many times by crowds of young people in recent years in Medjugorje, Yugoslavia.

Accordingly, it seems reasonable to conclude that Jesus did live again after being killed by crucifixion. It also seems that he appeared with a spiritual body at least on the road to Emmaus and in Jerusalem. It remains mysterious that no trace of Jesus' body has ever been discovered despite the tremendous motivation for those opposed to the resurrection to produce it.

But what does the resurrection signify to Christians? It provides assurance that when we die, it will not be the end of our existence because we may continue to live in another form of life. Furthermore, it may constitute God's seal of approval of Jesus as the Revealer of God to man and of God's will for man.

Jesus conspicuously attacked the commercialism of the Temple, and taught openly there. In short, did Jesus intend to precipitate his own death by his visit to and actions in Jerusalem? Or did he visit Jerusalem for the Passover festival and was then overwhelmed by the unexpected events? He may simply have fled from Herod's domain to Jerusalem, fearing the same fate as John the Baptist but there is weightier evidence that he travelled to Jerusalem because he intended to die there. For example, the Christians would hardly invent Jesus' castigation of Peter as Satan for having challenged Jesus' prophecy of his suffering and death! Outside Jerusalem, Jesus foretells his fate, "I have a baptism to be baptized with..." (Luke 12:50), and asks the ambitious sons of Zebedee, "Are you able to drink the cup that I drink...?" (Mark 10:38.)

Assuming, therefore, that his death was self-sought, what did he intend to achieve by it?

Jesus expected God to impose his cosmic Kingdom on the world in the very near future, but before God could introduce it, there had to be the pre-Messianic tribulation in which people would be persecuted for their sins (Mark 13:19). Jesus also expected this quickly. On sending the apostles on their first mission, he says, "When they persecute you in one town, flee to the next... for you will not have gone through all the towns of Israel before the Son of man comes." (meaning the Judge of the Elect). (Mark 10:23.) And yet, they were not persecuted and the Son did not come as the Judge. Meditation on this and on the 'Suffering Servant' of Isaiah 53 convinced Jesus that since the suffering of people generally, did not happen, God must intend that he, Jesus, must suffer instead on their behalf. So he says that he came to serve and to "give his life as a ransom for many", and at the last Supper he compares the broken bread to his body to be broken for many, and the wine to his blood to be shed for many. He intended that his death and suffering, instead of people generally, should satisfy the demands of Satan for the punishment of mankind for its sins thereby enabling God to bring in his direct rule of the world.

Jesus also expected that after his suffering and death he would return as the Son of God to judge the people's eligibility for the Kingdom. That, I suggest, is the theological reason why Jesus died. But it is arguable that Jesus' death did not achieve what he intended since God's rule in the world now manifests itself no more than it did before his death; evil still abounds. Nor has he returned speedily as Son of man to judge readiness for that Kingdom.

Consequently, our next question must be: What unintended results did Jesus' death achieve?

Christians have believed from early times that Jesus' death reconciled God to man, that it effected an 'atonement', i.e. at-one-ment, between man and God. The main form of this theory is that Jesus' death, like the sacrifice of an animal in the Temple, took away man's sin. This form is evidenced by John the Baptist's exclamation at Jesus, "Here is the Lamb of God who takes away the sins of the world!" (John 1:29), and by Paul's words, "Christ, our paschal lamb has been sacrificed," (1 Corinthians 5:7). The symbol of a lamb is appropriate since Jesus died on the cross at the time the lambs for the Passover meal were being slaughtered in the Temple. A glance at a daily paper shows, however, that the world is still steeped in sin. Most forms of atonement ideas can be seen developing from Jesus' own belief that in his death he was bearing the sins of others. The idea of Jesus' death effecting a 'redemption' from sin for us relates to Jesus' description of himself as a ransom for many, i.e. Satan took him as hostage so that mankind could be 'bought out' of the penalty for our sins (Mark 10:45). Yet we do still suffer and perhaps rightly so in the unhappiness which our sins inflict on us as well as others. The deficiency of these theories of atonement is that they necessitate belief in a God who demands the unjust suffering of an innocent man before he will be reconciled to his creatures–a stark contrast to the loving God preached by Jesus.

Nevertheless, it is arguable that Jesus' death and suffering did, in fact, secure at least two momentous achievements even though they were not his avowed aim. By his voluntary suffering and death, Jesus gave mankind an objective lesson in how a man who truly loves God and thereby His neighbour will be strengthened by God to perform any task (regardless of how daunting it is) which that man believes God wants him to do. The failure of the expected cosmic Kingdom and of the judging Son of God to arrive supports the view that Jesus was mistaken about God's plan. But the mistake is irrelevant to the achievement. The point is that *believing* it was His Father's will that he should suffer for this purpose, he obeyed. Being human, he feared pain and death as we do and pleaded, "Abba, Father... remove this cup from me", but added the imperishable words of obedience, "Yet not what I will but what thou wilt" (Mark 14:36).

The second unintended achievement of Jesus flows from the first. Many would-be Christians are perplexed when they hear Christians speak of 'salvation' and 'being saved' in several different ways. But one meaning is crystal clear to those who have been 'saved' from committing many sins by remembrance of the supreme example of one who was obedient to the extent of being nailed on a Cross believing it to be His Father's will.

Are these God-intended reasons why Jesus died?

"The kingdom of God has come near" (Mark 1:15). But where and when?

These questions and the nature of the kingdom has been a cause of difference between scholars and division between churches. For Jesus seems to speak of two kinds of kingdom and of varying time-scales for their arrival.

He preaches both about an external, cosmic kingdom and an internal kingdom. Even if we reject the Marcan Apocalypse (Ch.13) as being the product of the early church, there is still much evidence to show that Jesus confidently expected God to finally intervene to judge the world and to impose—by force—his kingdom in the sense of kingly rule. The 'Q' Apocalypse (Luke 17:22–37), for example, stresses this belief in the suddenness of the kingdom's arrival, as does the theme of several parables (e.g. the foolish virgins), and the criterion of eligibility for that kingdom is described in the parable of the great assize.

But Jesus also taught that His Father's kingdom prevails whenever God reigns in the human heart through obedience to his will, as revealed in the commandments old and new. He preached, "The kingdom of God is within you."(Luke 17:21).

Admittedly, Luke's Greek word 'entos' can also be translated 'in the midst of', although Luke usually employs another Greek preposition (en meso) for 'in the midst of'. Whichever translates more correctly Jesus' Aramaic here, he is clearly referring to an internal non–cosmic kingdom. In the parable, of the Seed (Mark 4:26–29) Jesus compares the imperceptible growth of God's kingly rule in the human heart with a seed which sprouts and grows while the farmer sleeps and rises, unconscious of the change. In the parable of the

Mustard Seed which follows, Jesus likens the spread of the kingdom among the hearts of men to the mustard seed which starts as the smallest seed but which grows to become the greatest shrub. And in the parable of the leaven (Luke 13:20–21) he shows how the attitudes of the kingdom can gradually permeate a man's life just as a small amount of yeast can slowly leaven three measures of meal.

Yet are not the two kinds of kingdoms discussed by Jesus, the external and the internal, inconsistent? If the kingdom depends on the state of the human heart, how can it also be an external cosmic revolution? Perhaps the two concepts are compatible if they are treated sequentially, i.e. following each other. God's internal kingdom exists here and now, in that, He rules like a king in the hearts of those who are obedient to His will. But the kingdom will prevail universally when on the 'Day of the Lord', God imposes his will by violent act over the whole world.

However, we can justly consider the citizens of his Father's internal kingdom to be those who, at the Judgment initiating the cosmic Kingdom, would emerge as 'sheep' rather than 'goats' (Matthew 25:31).

There is also uncertainty over the time of arrival of the external kingdom. In the case of the internal kingdom, the position seems plain that the kingdom arrives gradually as in the parable of the Seed to the extent that a man excludes self and devotes his life to the demands of the kingdom, repenting and accepting the kingdom with the innocence of a child and helping others as the Good Samaritan did. However, the parables of the Hidden Treasure and of the Pearl of Great Price (Matthew 13:44–45) suggest that some people may be required to surrender everything immediately in order to enter the kingdom. Monks/nuns and missionaries may be so obligated.

In the case of the external kingdom, Jesus' intimation about its time of arrival range from indications that it has already arrived to an expression of ignorance as to 'when this is to be'. This fluctuating teaching appears to indicate change in Jesus' thought as follows:

At the outset of his ministry Jesus preached, as mentioned above, that the kingdom had come near. Indeed, C. H. Dodd argued for 'realised eschatology'—that Jesus believed that the kingdom had already arrived. This view is supported by Jesus' saying, "But if it is by the finger of God that I cast out demons then the kingdom of God has come upon you." (Luke 11:20). Again, Jesus proclaims that the Isaianic prophesy of good news for the poor and release for captives etc. has been fulfilled that day (Luke 4:21; Matthew 11:4). However, since the cataclysmic physical events prophesied in the Apocalypses (wars, earthquakes etc.) had not occurred, the exorcisms, healings and good news of Jesus' ministry should probably only be seen as anticipatory signs of the external kingdom.

At the second stage of his thought, Jesus sees the kingdom as postponed but only for a brief period. Thus on sending out the Twelve on their first missionary journey, He instructs them, "When they persecute you in one town, flee to the next; for truly I say to you, you will not have gone through all the towns of Israel before the Son of Man comes." (Matthew 10:23). But by the time the Twelve returned, the persecutions which Jesus had represented as the Messianic woes preceding the kingdom had not taken place. According to Albert Schweitzer, the non-fulfilment of that prophesy caused Jesus to review the time when he would be dining at the Messianic banquet in the Kingdom. Thus he prophesied, "I have earnestly desired to eat this Passover with you before I suffer, for I tell you I shall not eat it until it is fulfilled in the kingdom of God" (Luke 22:15–16) and "from now on I shall not drink of the fruit of the vine until the kingdom of God comes" (Luke 22:18)

To summarise, it seems that Jesus' various estimates of the time of arrival of the external cosmic kingdom went awry except to the extent that the wondrous cures and other works of his ministry can be interpreted as 'trailers' of the kingdom . But as he declared, the internal kingdom had 'come near' nay, was actually present. Like the mustard seed, it was sown in the apostles and has since blossomed throughout the ages in countless hearts.

Chapter 3
The Supernatural

"I Form Light and Create Darkness, I Make Weal and Create Woe" (Isaiah 45:7)

Several doctrines involve the supernatural in ways which liberal Christians and aspirant followers of Jesus may find difficult.

Good Christian Men Rejoice!

Good Christian men rejoice with heart and soul and voice! Yes, but at what in particular in regard to Christmas? Surely, at the fact that Jesus of Nazareth was born at all.

His birth may not have occurred on the day that is 25th December in our calendar. That day, first celebrated by Christians in the West about 300 CE, was probably chosen because the pagan festivals of Mithras and Saturn occurred around the winter solstice. (Luke's shepherds would have been watching their flocks in the fields between November and March.)

Rather do the followers of Jesus rejoice that a man who, by his words, deeds and self-sacrificial death, was able to reveal God's nature and will for man, did indeed enter this world at some point. But the gratitude that he was born into this world does not oblige Christians to accept all the Gospel stories about his birth. In fact, only Matthew and Luke relate the birth of Jesus; Mark and John are silent. The incidents surrounding his birth, which Matthew and Luke respectively recount, are surprisingly different. For example, only Matthew mentions the Magi and the family's flight to Egypt, and only Luke describes the shepherds' visit to the manger. However, they all agree on the virgin birth or, more accurately, the virginal conception. This supernatural tenet of creedal Christianity deserves our attention.

The evidence given by Matthew is that before the betrothed Mary and Joseph came together, she was found to be with child by the Holy Spirit, that Joseph was persuaded in a dream not to divorce her, and that he did not 'know' her (carnally) until she had borne a son (1:18–25).

Luke asserts that the angel Gabriel announced to a virgin, Mary, that she would conceive and bear a son, Jesus. To Mary's enquiry as to how this could be since she had not a husband (Greek, "I do not know a man"), the angel replied that the Holy Spirit would come upon her and the power of the Most High would overshadow her (1:26–35).

Against this evidence of Matthew and Luke supporting a virginal conception, there is substantial counter-evidence. An argument from silence is not usually strong, but it is strange that apart from those two Gospels there is no explicit reference to a virgin birth in the New Testament. Since such a birth would have been a persuasive argument to Hellenistic Gentiles for Jesus' divine origin, its omission from the Acts of the Apostles and from Paul's letters must be classed as some counter-evidence. Indeed, in Romans 1:4 (written before the Gospels), we read, "...his Son who was descended from David according to the flesh..." Joseph's paternity is probably implied here, since he was of the House of David.

More counter-evidence arises from the frequency with which a virgin birth is ascribed to both secular and spiritual heroes in the ancient world. In world religions, Buddha, Krishna and Zoroaster's son; in mythology, Perseus and Romulus; in history the Pharaohs, Alexander the Great and Augustus Caesar; and in philosophy, Plato and Apollonius were all credited with a virgin mother.

The most formidable and obvious obstacle arrayed against the Evangelists' evidence is the biological law that in the human species, male sperm is necessary for female conception. Admittedly, the critical spirit of historical enquiry demands that any event which appears to breach the laws of nature must be tested on its evidence—not precluded by any dogma with regards to the universality of the natural laws (R.G. Collingwood). But such is the regularity of those laws, that strong and consistent evidence is surely needed to prove a suspension of them.

Here, the evidence for the virginal conception, adduced by only two of the Evangelists and opposed by much counter-evidence, may not be thought strong enough to establish a breach of those laws. An alternative explanation of the assertions of a virginal conception could be that they were provoked by the belief in Jesus' deity which followed the resurrection; it may have been thought unsuitable that the 'Son of God' should have been tainted, in origin, by the cultic impurity of human copulation (Leviticus 15:18). Support for this early Christian desire for a virginal conception was found in the LXX (Greek) translation of Isaiah 7:14 where God tells Ahaz, "Behold a virgin shall conceive and bear a son, and shall call his name Immanuel." And these words are also quoted by Matthew (1:23). But the Greeks have mistranslated the word for 'virgin' in the Hebrew which is 'almah' and normally means a girl who has reached the age of puberty and is thus marriageable—this Hebrew word is neutral as to whether the girl is a virgin or not (The Hebrew word 'bethula' indicates virginity).

So the next question is—Who was Jesus' father?

In 248 CE, Origen, an early Christian scholar and teacher, reported statements of his heathen opponent, Celsus, that Miriam (the Jewish form of Mary) was divorced by her husband, a carpenter, for adultery with a Roman soldier, Panthera, and that she later bore Panthera's child, Jesus, in secrecy. In Rabbinic works of 3rd and 5th century CE (the Tosefta and the Jerusalem Talmud), Rabbis of the 2nd century refer to Jesus as 'the son of Panthera'. Thus, the alternatives are that either Joseph or Panthera was Jesus' father. The evidence favouring Joseph's paternity is that both Matthew and Luke report that he was betrothed to Mary. 'Betrothed' in the Gospels means 'engaged to be married'. Betrothal in Jewish law had more legal consequences than in English law, since from the moment of engagement, the woman was treated as if she were married; the union could only be severed by divorce and unfaithfulness was deemed adultery. Yet the wife continued to live at her family home until the second formal act, the transfer of the bride to the husband's family home which took place usually a year after the betrothal. Although some customs in Galilee were different from those in Judea, it is implicit in rulings of the Rabbis reported in the Mishnah (compiled in 200 CE) that relations between a betrothed couple were more relaxed in Judea than in Galilee and that in Judea, the couple might occasionally be alone during the betrothal period. Matthew reports the family as going to Nazareth in Galilee only after their return from Egypt—he places his nativity story in Bethlehem of Judea. Thus despite the Gospel's denials, it is clearly possible that Joseph and Mary did consummate their union during the betrothal period.

Since the statements of Celsus and the Rabbis about Panthera may have been motivated by hostility, the main evidence favouring Panthera's paternity is the report of Matthew alone, that Joseph initially intended to divorce Mary 'quietly'. This could be affected by serving a bill of divorcement (a git) on Mary (which only required two witnesses) rather than by complaining publicly to the elders about her adultery, which might have involved a severe penalty for Mary (Deuteronomy 22:13–21).

But since Matthew's evidence of Joseph's intention to divorce Mary is not corroborated by Luke, I think that the cumulative weight of (1) the corroborated evidence of Mary's conception during her betrothal to Joseph; (2) the tracing of Jesus' ancestors through Joseph in both the Matthean and the Lucan genealogies and in Romans (1:4); (3) the absence of any mention of any irregularity about Jesus' birth elsewhere in the New Testament (except, perhaps, at Mark (6:3)), and (4) the Rabbinic evidence of access produces a preponderance of testimony in favour of Joseph's biological fatherhood of Jesus.

Yet is there any less cause for rejoicing if Jesus was conceived in this normal way? The natural reproduction of the species is itself a miracle in the true sense of something wonderful and does not need the addition of a supernatural element (i.e. beyond the laws of nature) to demonstrate the glory of God's creation. And it detracts no whit from the status of Jesus or the motherhood of Mary that Jesus' father was Joseph.

The Resurrection

Did Jesus live again after being killed by crucifixion and, if so, in what way?

"If Christ has not been raised... then your faith has been in vain" (1 Corinthians 15:14). So wrote Paul to the Christians at Corinth and this has remained a cardinal belief of Jesus' followers. There are several reports in the Gospels that support this belief.

For example, all four Gospel writers say that those who visited Jesus' tomb found that it was empty. To rebut any allegations that the tomb was empty because Jesus had risen from the dead, the story that the disciples had stolen the body arose. Matthew states that some of the guards told the chief priests everything that had happened and the chief priests paid the soldiers to say that his disciples had stolen the body while they were asleep. According to Matthew, the chief priests, recollecting that Jesus had promised that he would rise again after 3 days, feared that the disciples would remove the body to fulfil this promise. So they asked Pilate for permission to make the tomb secure, which they did by sealing it with a stone (Matthew 26:62–66).

Luke states that on the following day Cleopas and another disciple were walking to Emmaus and were joined by Jesus whom they did not recognise until he blessed, broke and gave them bread. They returned to Jerusalem and told the disciples who informed them that Jesus had appeared to Peter. At this moment Jesus appeared and they thought they were seeing a ghost but he showed them his hands and feet and ate broiled fish in their presence .He commissioned them and led them out to Bethany, where he was carried up to a cloud. John adds that Thomas did not believe that Jesus had appeared but a week later Jesus appeared again when the doors were shut and he invited Thomas to feel his hands and side. This convinced him. John reports a third appearance on the beach by the sea, where Jesus distributed bread and fish and talked at length with his disciples.

These incidents, if authentic, constitute strong evidence that Jesus lived again and appeared in some form to the disciples. Indeed, Paul states that he appeared to over 500 people. As indicated above, the evidence conflicts over whether he appeared in his human body or whether he possessed a spiritual form. The reports that suggest that Jesus showed his disciples his hands and feet on two occasions and ate with them on the road to Emmaus, attest to his possession of a physical human body.

The Jews of that time believed that there was no change in bodies after death—as the earth received them, so it would restore them.

"For I Am the Lord, Your Healer" (Exodus 15:26)

The authenticity of most of the Gospel reports of Jesus' healings seems firmly grounded. Admittedly, there was motivation for Christians to accept the stories of Jesus' healing miracles, since healing works were expected of the Messiah as a sign of true Messiahship. But the large number of reports of healings and the vivid details vouch for his healing ministry. And it is unlikely that Christians would have invented the cures which involved disputes with the Pharisees over work on the Sabbath.

The Latin derivation of 'miracle' (miraculum) simply means something wonderful but the word has been used in religious language to signify an event which transcends the laws of nature, i.e. is supernatural. Thus the divinity of Jesus has been supported on the ground that he effected 'miracles' of healing in the sense of cures which over-rode the known laws of biology.

Most Christians would agree that all healing is done—directly or indirectly—by God who created the human body and re-creates it by means of chemicals derived from the created earth and by the skills of surgeons, physicians and nurses whom he also formed.

Indeed, the body has built-in repair facilities, blood congeals over a cut and new skin forms. Broken bones sometimes knit themselves together and the outer skin of the whole body is renewed at least once a year.

But Jesus is reputed to have cured medical conditions which do not self-repair: leprosy, haemorrhage, blindness, spinal curvature, dropsy, withered hand, dumbness, deafness, paralysis and epilepsy. In several cures, Jesus commends the faith of the patient. To the woman with a haemorrhage he says, "Your faith has made you well" (Mark 5:34). He says the same to the formerly blind Bartimaeus (Mark 10:52) and declares to the centurion, "Not even in Israel have I found such faith" (Matthew 8:10). The Greek word root used by the Evangelists in these contexts for 'faith' and 'belief' is 'pist' which means trust, not creedal conviction. Jesus means that it is the trust or confidence possessed by the patient in God's ability to cure him through Jesus' ministration which has enabled the cure.

In contrast to healings, in the case of the expulsion of demons or unclean spirits (exorcisms) this trust does not feature except in Mark (9:23) where, before expelling a dumb and deaf spirit, Jesus says to the patient's father, "All things are possible to him who believes."

In the other cases, the demoniac is usually hostile, and Jesus' expulsion of the demon is contrary to the demoniac's wishes. In Mark (1:24), the demoniac asks if Jesus has come to destroy him and at 5:7 adjures Jesus not to torment him. Jesus does not mention the patient's faith in every healing (e.g. Peter's mother-in-law at Matthew 8:14–15, but the several cases where faith is mentioned may suggest that this was an element in all his healings (as opposed to exorcisms). Thus Mark reports that when Jesus taught at Nazareth and the people took offence at him, he only healed a few sick people and he marvelled at their unbelief (6:1–6).

That faith or spiritual healing is effective, in some cases, is supported by the successes of modern spiritual healers — the work of Harry Edwards, for example, is well attested.

Most healers acknowledge that, although some receive the assistance of intermediary spirit 'guides', the healing power emanates from God. But does the faith healing of Jesus and others involve any breach of the laws of biology established at creation as part of the laws of nature? In other words, does it involve the supernatural? Christians traditionally treat Jesus' healings as miracles in the sense that God here suspends or breaks the laws which He established at creation. This constitutes an obstacle for those who wish to follow Jesus but are deterred by the supernatural happenings they think they are required to accept in order to become a Christian.

Cannot this obstacle be removed? The influence of mind over matter is generally acknowledged in the way in which our state of mind influences the state of our body—'mens agitat molem'—this is called psychosomatic. In times of stress, for example, our digestion and appetite are affected, and severe anxiety can cause stomach ulcers. Conversely, Jesus attributes the success of his healing of the patient's body to the positive state of his mind, "Your faith (trust) has made you whole." (Mark 5:3–4). The body has reacted benignly to the patient's confident state of mind. The reverse also applies in that our bodily condition can influence our state of mind. Tiredness of body can produce lassitude of mind.

This interaction between the mind and the body is surely part of the laws of nature (biology) so that faith healing is not supernatural, hence, not a 'miracle' in the religious sense of the word. This does not undermine the wonder of Jesus' cures; to inspire in the patient such trust that he will be cured demands a vibrant charismatic personality and a susceptibility to be a channel of God's healing power.

However, on this psychosomatic understanding of Jesus' cures a query arises in the case of healings at a distance. For example, how can the centurion's son (or slave) in Matthew (8:5–13) have formed the necessary trust in Jesus' power to heal when, being 'at the point of death', he had never met Jesus? Yet healing by prayer in the absence of the patient is accomplished by modern faith healers and there are other reported cases nearly contemporary with Jesus. According to the Talmud, R. Hanina b. Dosa, around the end of the first century, prayed in his upper room for the absent son of R. Gamaliel who immediately recovered from his fever (Berakoth, 34b). Similarly, animals cannot perhaps form the necessary mental state of trust in a faith healer, yet instances of such healings are also attested. Do the absent patient and the animal somehow know and have confidence that their suffering is about to cease?

Can Demons Inhabit a Human Body?

The presence of demons (unclean spirits) inside the bodies of afflicted persons is a basic premise of their expulsion by Jesus. He asserted, "If I by the finger of God have cast out demons then the kingdom of God has come upon you." (Luke 11:20). But can another living entity reside in the body of a human being? Certainly, microbes and other living physical organisms enter our bodies, but can an incorporeal entity do so?

We have the evidence of both ancient and modern witnesses that it can. The Gospels report several instances where Jesus expelled a resident demon. In Mark (1:25), Jesus commands the demon, "Be silent, and come out of him!", and in Mark (5:8), "Come out of the man, you unclean spirit!"

In the parable in Luke (11:24–26) Jesus describes how, when the unclean spirit had "gone out of a man", he decided to return; he found the house put in order, and so he brought seven more evil spirits who entered and dwelt there.

Again, Josephus, the Jewish historian writing in Rome about 93 CE, testified, "I have seen a certain Eleazar, a countryman of mine, in the presence of Vespasian (the Roman emperor) free men possessed by demons, and this was the manner of the cure: he put a ring through the nose of the possessed man which had under its seal one of the roots prescribed by Solomon, and then, as the man smelled it, he drew out the demon through his nostrils. When the man at once fell down, he adjured the demon never to come back into him, speaking Solomon's name and the incantations which he had composed. Then Eleazar placed a cup of water a little way off and commanded the demon as it went out of the man, to overturn it. And when this was done..." (Antiquities VIII, 46). We must allow for some decoration of an ancient story; but it is evidence that exorcisms occurred (cf. Acts 5:16; 8:7).

Exorcism is also frequently practised in modern times. Leslie Weatherhead quotes from Mildred Cable's book, 'The Fulfilment of a Dream', "Our first woman patient in Hwacha Opium Refuge' became interested in the Gospel and on her return home destroyed her idols, reserving, however, the idol shrines which she placed in her son's room. Her daughter-in-law who occupied this room desired to become a Christian. About six months later we were fetched to see this girl who was said to be possessed by a demon. The girl was chanting the weird minor chant of the possessed. It seemed as though the demon used the organs of speech of the victim for the conveyance of its own voice. She, by her violence, terrorised the community. We endeavoured to calm her and asked her to join us in repeating, 'Lord Jesus, save me'. When she had done so, we commanded the demon to leave her, whereupon her body trembled and she sneezed some 50 or 60 times, then suddenly came to herself and resumed her work." (Psychology, Religion and Healing', 1951, p .102).

Michael Green writes, "The most sensational, and one of the earliest experiences I had was when entering a room where a possessed person was standing (and raving). The person screeched aloud and shrank to the wall at the arrival of another Christian. I felt an immediate, almost palpable sense of evil, went up to the person and commanded the evil thing that was causing the trouble, to name itself. This it did, to my great surprise. Then, having nothing but the Gospels to go on, I commanded it by its name to come out. It did—and the person crashed to the ground." (I believe in Satan's downfall 1981, p.133).

Against this evidence, ancient and modern, that demons are expelled from within the human body, stand the views of psychiatrists. The majority of psychiatrists would probably treat the experience of demons as wholly within the patient's selfhood an emanation from his brain. It is a psychosis in which the patient is unable to separate fantasy from reality. Carl Jung asserted that, "From the psychological point of view demons are nothing other than intruders from the unconscious, spontaneous irruptions of unconscious complexes into the continuity of the conscious process. Complexes are comparable to demons which fitfully harass our thoughts and actions; hence in antiquity and the Middle Ages acute neurotic disturbances were conceived as (daemonic) possession."

The psychiatrist, Derek Anton-Stephens, writing in 'The Christian Parapsychologist' (March 1994), explains that the experiences of many people (not only psychiatric patients) would be attributed to demons if modern psychiatry did not exist. They experience an alien 'something' which controls their bodily and mental activity. It may be an intruding voice, a touch, inserted thoughts or a vision, but always 'alienation', being influenced by something 'alien' or 'other' to oneself.

Anton-Stephens admits that the experience of alienation can often be shown to be linked with physical disorder, but not always. He writes, "An illness can be shown to cause the alienation, and, of course, not all hysterics and schizophrenics feel alienated."

Anton-Stephens raises another important argument against the view confining cases of alienation or possession to mental illness. He notes that, "more men and women than is perhaps generally realised, e.g. mystics, mediums and clairvoyants, experience the same alienation as mentally ill patients yet do not require the care of psychiatrists." Their 'voices', 'thought intrusions' and 'visions' are basically the same as those of schizophrenics and hysterics. So the conclusion that mental illness is the only cause of symptoms of alienation or possession, appears invalid. But this argument does not prove that the alienation is caused by a demon or force external to the selfhood of the patient, for he may be of sound mind yet simply mistaken in his view that he is affected by an incorporeal entity alien to him.

Perhaps the concept that a person can be influenced to the extent of being controlled by an alien 'force' is correct and it is only the view that personifies the force and sees it as literally residing in the body or mind of the human, which is mistaken. Christians refer to the 'indwelling' Holy Spirit and the 'receiving of the Spirit at baptism (Acts 19:1) but the meaning is surely that God's power is influencing the Christian rather than that a spiritual entity is residing in him. Instead of describing the termination of the alienation or the exorcism in terms of 'expelling a demon' perhaps we should—today—understand the process as the summoning of a greater force (the power of God or the personality of Jesus or other charismatic being) to dominate over the pre-existing force influencing the victim. Thus in Mark (1:44) the man with an unclean spirit cried out, "What have you to do with us, Jesus of Nazareth? Have you come to destroy us?" (cf.5:7).

Whether the concept is expressed in the language of 'residing in' the person or simply 'influencing' him hardly matters; the question of fundamental importance is whether a person's mind or body can be affected by an incorporeal, spiritual or psychic force or entity (in addition to God). Thus the substance of the reports of Jesus' exorcisms is probably correct, he did terminate the influence of an alien force on the patient's selfhood but the form in which the action was described, the literal driving out of a demon from within the patient's body, was incorrect. So when we read in Mark (1:26) that the unclean spirit convulsed him, cried out with a loud voice and came out of him, we should probably understand that Jesus' rebuke of the alien force dominated it, that the man suffered trauma in the mental conflict involved, and was then freed from its effect. Again, when the demon says to Jesus, "I know who you are", we should interpret this as the speech of the patient influenced in his thought by the alien force.

The weight of the ancient and modern evidence of exorcisms (of which we have cited examples), when added to the points raised by Anton-Stephens seem to outweigh the medical evidence that the alienation or possession experience is produced only by the malfunctioning (psychosis) of the patient's brain. That alien incorporeal forces can influence and even control the human mind seems a probability.

Did the Death of Jesus Effect an Atonement for Sin?

A stumbling block to following Jesus may be experienced by some in the apparent centrality in mainstream Christianity of the doctrine of atonement. This doctrine is illustrated in John the Baptist's calling of Jesus, "The Lamb of God who takes away the sin of the world." (John 1:29). The reference to the lamb, recalls the transfer to a lamb of the sins of the people on the Jewish Day of Atonement. Thus the effect of Jesus' death is explained as his taking away the sin of the world by suffering his own death to free people generally from bearing punishment for their sins.

The view that Jesus believed that part of the purpose of his death was to suffer in himself, the punishment due to humanity generally for its sins, is primarily supported by his saying at Mark (10:45) and at the Last Supper. At Mark (10:45), Jesus is reported to say, "The Son of man came to give his life as a ransom for many." (In Aramaic 'many' in this context could mean people generally). The 'ransom' paid with the death of one man there is intended to liberate the rest of humanity from paying for their sins. Matthew copies the saying in 20:28 but Luke omits it. Some scholars have doubted that Jesus uttered these words, arguing that they were a later addition.

At the Last Supper, Jesus is reported by Paul as having said about the bread, "This is my body which is (broken) for you." (1 Corinthians 11:24), and in Mark (14:24) Jesus is reported to refer to the wine as, "my blood of the covenant which is poured out for many."

As discussed below (pp. 66-8), the covenant here may be the new covenant mentioned in Jeremiah which provides that God will forgive their iniquity and remember their sins no more. (31:31–34). Furthermore, Jesus may have seen himself as the 'suffering servant' of whom Isaiah says, "He bore the sin of many." (Isaiah 53:12).

Standing against this evidence that Jesus believed he was to suffer for the sins of the people is his teaching that people would in fact suffer for their sins themselves. In Mark (9:43) Jesus warns that it is better to enter life maimed than "with two hands to go to hell, to the unquenchable fire."

In the parable of Dives and Lazarus (Luke 16:19–31) the rich man is described as being in Hades in torment from the flame. In another parable, the Sheep and the Goats (Matthew 25:31–46), the 'goats' who did not help the needy, are banished to the eternal fire. However, the two views are not inconsistent, Jesus did teach that people would suffer for their sins, but he may have realised later that it was the will of God that he should bear the punishment, instead. In my view the balance of evidence indicates that Jesus did believe that his death would take away sins, but then the question arises, was his belief mistaken? The prophets of Israel (vide Isaiah at 1:18–20) and Jesus himself had already stressed God's willingness to forgive on genuine repentance (e.g. the parable of the Prodigal Son and the Lord's Prayer). Indeed, God had forgiven many penitents before the time of Jesus, as in the case of David (2 Samuel 12:13). It is, therefore, arguable that it was unnecessary for Jesus to die to effect the forgiveness of the sins of the people.

Whatever be the nature of his divine status, Jesus was fully human, and so was capable of making mistakes (e.g. his teaching that the external Kingdom of God would arrive very soon—Matthew 10:23).

Perhaps the strongest evidence favouring a mistake by Jesus over the consequences of his death is that Yahweh is a loving and just God, and it is entirely inconsistent with this

47

character that he should want an innocent man to be killed before he would forego punishment of the guilty. Hastings Rashdall wrote, "No doctrine of the atonement can be genuinely Christian, which contradicts a feature of that teaching—as fundamental as the truth—that God is a loving Father who will pardon sin upon the sole condition of true repentance."

So what was the benefit conferred on the world by Jesus' death, by his body '(broken) for you'? I suggest that Jesus thereby gave to mankind the supreme example of obedience to the will of God in that he suffered death because he thought (albeit mistakenly) that it was his Father's wish. In Mark (14:36), Jesus is reported to pray, "Abba, Father, all things are possible to thee; remove this cup from me; yet not what I will, but what thou wilt." That example has doubtlessly enabled many to convert from sin and pursue a changed lifestyle based on his teaching. Jesus' death did not literally 'take away the sin of the world' because sin has been as evident in the world since his death as it was before. But his death suffered, in obedience, provided the inspiration which can encourage a person to overcome temptation to sin. Thus the aspirant Christian may find himself able to follow Jesus, untroubled by the conceptual difficulties surrounding the traditional doctrine of the atonement.

But the belief that the death of Jesus, did in some way take away the sins of the world, remains a central element in creeds and Christian worship, generally.

Does God Act Now and at the End?

Most Christians would agree that Jesus proclaimed a Kingdom of God which reigns in the heart of a person when he obeys his Father's will as revealed by the prophets of Israel, and especially by Jesus. Sayings such as 'The Kingdom of God is within you' (Luke 17:21) and parables such as the Secret Seed and the Mustard Seed (Mark 4:26–32) and the Leaven (Matthew 13:33) testify to this aspect of the Kingdom. But Jesus, like the prophets of Israel, taught also of an external Kingdom of God which would come when, on the Day of the Lord, God would impose his reign over the world, externally and cosmically (e.g. Zechariah 14:1–9; Mark 13).

Yet does God intervene in the physical and external world? If He does not, the prophecies of that cosmic Kingdom, and Jesus' claimed anticipation of it in his own healings (Luke 11:20) were in vain.

No theist would doubt that God acted in the creation of that physical world. He created the universe, and at the same time established the laws of nature (e.g. physics, chemistry and biology) which control its operations. Whether that creation was by Big Bang and subsequent Darwinian evolution, or was completed in 7 days as Genesis relates, does not affect the enquiry.

But, having acted in creation, does God continue to act in the world? It is arguable that He does so in the following ways:

1. He acts by maintaining the life force, by continuing the cycle of the seasons, the days and nights, the course of the heavenly bodies. But are not these regularities the result of the laws of nature which God established at creation?

2. The Bible constantly asserts that God acts in history, and most significantly in the 'salvation' events of Judaism and Christianity. In the Exodus, God released Israel from slavery in Egypt and by the Crucifixion and Resurrection of Jesus, God freed men from slavery to sin and assured them of eternal life. Yet are not the Exodus and the Crucifixion also interpretable as events caused by the free-will of the participants rather than actions of God? And is not the Resurrection also intelligible, as the activity of the spiritual body separated after death from the physical body, according to laws of nature of which we are at present imperfectly aware?

3. Paradoxically, God intervenes externally in the world through His internal Kingdom in that He influences the thoughts of men through dreams, visions, prayers, Bible study or conscience. To cause thought is to affect the brain cells, therefore, God does act in the physical world although this seems only light impact upon it.

The Feeding of the Five Thousand (Mark 6:35-44)

In this well-known story five loaves and two fish were found more than sufficient to feed five thousand men, for twelve baskets of food were left over. And Matthew mentions that women and children were fed in addition to the men. There is good evidence for this happening since all the Gospels, including John's, give a similar version, although, Matthew and Luke are probably relying on Mark's version.

Several different views have been taken of the authenticity of this apparent multiplication of the loaves and fishes. Many see it as a miracle in the sense that it occurred supernaturally, in that, contrary to the laws of nature, Jesus converted the loaves and fishes into enough food to feed 5,000 and more. This view has to be seriously considered, because we have the evidence of Mark that this is what it was–a miracle. In support of the historicity of Mark's story, the life-like details of Jewish origin which he includes, can be cited. But against the conclusion of a supernatural miracle, various points have been raised. It is pointed out that in his visionary temptations in the wilderness, Jesus was challenged, 'Tell these stones to become bread' (Matthew 4:3). And again, to prove his Sonship, he was invited by Satan to throw himself down from the Temple roof since the angels would take care of him. Both of these temptations he resisted, presumably because he did not wish his powers to be used for theatrical self-glorification, but rather for the healing of others. This same approach would have prevented him, it is argued, from winning the crowd's admiration by magic with loaves. Yes, they were hungry but the provision of one meal was hardly an act of healing.

Further, the prophets of old were reported to have done amazing things, and Jesus was believed to be greater than them. Therefore, he must have done similar things, if not more. In 2 Kings (4:42–44), Elisha told his servant to give the prophetic party the twenty loaves of barley, which a man had brought them. His servant asked how this was to feed a hundred men. Elisha replied that the Lord had said they would eat and have some left. And so it turned out. In Jesus' case a smaller amount of food fed a much greater number, thus demonstrating his superiority.

But if the loaves and fish were not miraculously multiplied, what did happen? We cannot know. One proposal is that the example shown by the disciples of sharing their loaves and fish with others, so impressed the crowd that all who had brought food shared it with their neighbours. It's relevant here that when Jesus first saw the crowd, 'his heart went out to them, because they were like sheep without a shepherd' and he had much to teach them. The warmth of Jesus' compassion for the crowd and the ethical standards such as loving your neighbour which he may well have taught, may have inspired in them a generosity of heart which resulted in the sharing of food. Later, Mark relates a similar feeding, this time, 4,000 people with seven loaves and a few small fish.

What did Mark think Jesus was trying to teach through these feedings? In chapter 8, Mark reports the disciples as not understanding his purpose and being upbraided by Jesus for their obtuseness. Perhaps Jesus intended that the disciples and the crowd should understand that his Father would provide for their spiritual needs and more, if only they would turn to him and trust in him. And that perhaps is the message he sends to us today. Just as his Father provided manna for the Israelites in the wilderness, and he produced loaves and fishes in Galilee, so may he provide spiritual sustenance for us when we receive the bread and wine.

"Command These Stones to Become Loaves of Bread" (Mark 4:3)

Jesus refused to perform this supernatural act since he believed that his powers should be employed purely to advance the kingdom, and should not be used for personal glory. Thus he also refused the temptation to throw himself from the pinnacle of the Temple. Yet the Gospels report him raising the dead, walking on water, stilling the storm and feeding 5000 with five loaves and two fish. These reports of supernatural powers may not, however, be authentic. The people of the 1st century were addicted to magical wonders and there are many stories of similar magic being performed by religious or important characters. In the 1st century CE, Apollonius of Tyana is reported to have raised a young bride from the dead in circumstances very similar to the raising of the young man of Nain. It would not be surprising if the followers of Jesus wished to show their leader as accomplishing the same wonders and they may have embellished genuine incidents with impressive details. For example, the fact that Jesus was believed to cast out demons is supported by the allegation that he cast out demons through Beelzebub, the prince of demons (Mark 3:22) —there would have been no base for this claim if Jesus had not effected exorcisms. Apparently other religious people also exorcised in the name of Jesus which supports the reality of Jesus' own activity (Mark 9:38).

The Last Supper

The words and actions of Jesus at the Last Supper arguably do not involve the supernatural but Christians from the beginning interpreted them in a supernatural way. Paul in his first letter to the Corinthians written about 53 C.E. wrote that Jesus took bread, gave thanks, broke it and said, "This is my body that is broken for you. Do this in remembrance of me." (11:24). In Mark's version of the supper Jesus took bread, blessed and broke it and gave it to them saying, "take eat: this is my body." (14:22). The important difference is that in Paul's account Jesus said "this is my body" while breaking the bread, whereas in Mark's he said "take, eat: this is my body" while giving them the bread. The point made by Paul is that Jesus' body will be broken for them at the crucifixion 'just as this bread is broken', but in Mark the disciples are invited to eat Jesus' body. Against this understanding of Jesus's words lies the unlikelihood of such a request in the light of the Levitical prohibition of the consumption of human blood (17:12).

Jesus also gives the disciples the cup of wine to drink. This cup is described as "my blood of the covenant poured out for many" (Mark, 14:24) and "the new covenant in my blood". These phrases support the understanding of Jesus' words over the bread and wine as showing the sacrificial purpose of his coming death. It is perhaps unwise to place such weight on this slight change in Jesus' words but the variation does vitally affect the central rite of Christianity. For from earliest days the majority of Christians have interpreted the Last Supper as involving the transubstantiation of the bread and wine at every re-enactment of it at a mass or Holy Communion. If this transubstantiation does take place, it constitutes a supernatural event, but the New Testament evidence for the change in the bread and wine may be considered slender. Rather does it attest a call by Jesus for remembrance and "proclamation of the Lord's death until he comes." (1 Cor. 11:25–26).

Chapter 4
Law

Why Did Jesus Die?

The answer, historically and politically, is straightforward. The Jewish court, the Sanhedrin, before whom Jesus was charged with offences against Jewish law was composed of Sadducees and Pharisees and Jesus had alienated both parties. He had annoyed the Pharisees by attacking their interpretation of several of the written laws of Moses. Thus he disagreed with their comprehensive definition of "work" which was prohibited by the Sabbath commandment and he denied that it should prevent healing on that day. Also, he did not attach as much importance to the cultic law and the rules about diet and ritual cleanness as the Pharisees did. He alarmed the 'Sadducaic Establishment', i.e. the High Priest and the High Priestly families by gathering a popular following which they feared might provoke Pilate to intervene with troops and cancel the cosy 'concordat', whereby, control of Jewish affairs was delegated to the High Priest. Moreover, he infuriated the high priestly families by driving out of the Temple Court of the Gentiles, the businessmen who exchanged money and sold sacrificial animals there, for this expulsion threatened not only priestly authority but priestly purses.

So it is not surprising that these two parties combined to find Jesus guilty of an offence that carried the death penalty. It was probably blasphemy on the false ground that he had threatened to destroy the Temple. Blasphemy included the 'dishonour' of God and the Temple was linked with God's honour since his Name rested there. (In fact, Jesus had probably only prophesied that the Temple would be destroyed, which it was in 70 CE, by the Romans). However, the

Sanhedrin had no power to execute the death penalty since Rome reserved this to the praefectus (Pontius Pilate) as part of its 'imperium' over the province. Nevertheless, since they had shown their fellow-Jews that Jesus had committed blasphemy they would not be labelled 'quislings', when they next attempted to persuade Pilate to order his death instead.

Under the Roman provincial legal system, the accusation is not of a particular crime but of facts upon which the praefectus is invited to adjudicate. Since Pilate would not be interested in blasphemy against the Jewish God, the chief priests shrewdly alleged facts which endangered the very existence of Roman 'imperium'. Thus they complained—

"We found this man perverting our nation, and forbidding us to give tribute to Caesar, and claiming that he himself is Christ, a king." (Luke 23:3). Pilate found these claims to royalty from a reticent peasant hard to believe, but when the Jews threatened Pilate's own position saying, "If you let this man go, you are no friend of Caesar's" (John 19:12) he acquiesced and ordered Jesus' crucifixion.

Such were the immediate historical reasons for the death of Jesus but would Jesus have been so easily arrested and drawn into this final drama if he had not ridden into Jerusalem on a mule with the pretensions of royalty which that involved (cf. Absalom and Solomon)?

A scenario which fits the gospel evidence involves the conjunction of Jewish political and religious aspirations. The people (ha-amhaarez) were incensed by the heavy Roman taxation and disrespect for their faith and temple. Josephus wrote of frequent riots. Judas of Galilee rebelled in C.E.6 and Theudas in C.E.46. The people expected 'the last days' ('the day of the Lord') very soon when God would evict the Romans and Zion would dominate as predicted by the prophets (e.g. Joel 2). When they heard a preacher declaring that the time was fulfilled and the Kingdom was at hand (Mark1:14), they believed that the last days had arrived and they gave Jesus a triumphant entry to Jerusalem as the Danielic Son of Man and they tried to make him king (John 6:15). But they quickly realised that the Kingdom introduced by Jesus was a spiritual one and that his attitude towards the Romans was passive. Then their shouts changed from

'Hosanna!' to 'Crucify!'. However, some disciples still believed even after Jesus' Ascension that Jesus would 'restore the Kingdom' (Acts 1:6).

"You Shall Not Eat of the Fruit of the Tree That Is in the Middle of the Garden" (Genesis 3:3)

But Adam and Eve did eat, and disobeyed God's command. The story of the Garden of Eden is probably considered by many to be a myth, a fictional tale illustrating a truth. The truth, in this instance, is that humans have a propensity to disobey God's commands, and thus sin. This myth was interpreted by Tertullian, who lived from 160 to 230 CE, as teaching that the propensity to sin was passed down by Adam and Eve to all their descendants, i.e. all humanity. He wrote that, deceived by Satan (the serpent), the first man 'infected the whole race by his seed, making it the channel of damnation'. He thus believed that Adam received a pure human nature, but passed to his descendants a nature spoiled by an inclination to sin. He argued that the children of even Christians must be considered impure until they have been reborn by baptism. Some severe rules of the Church in the past have been based on this doctrine, such as denying a church burial to babies, if their original sin had not been washed away by baptism. The doctrine of original sin was accepted by most of the Church Fathers, including St. Augustine (354-430 CE), and passed into Christian orthodoxy.

Much doubt has been cast upon this doctrine in modern times, yet the doctrine gains considerable support from science. Evolution by natural selection or survival of the fittest means that those members of a species of animal who can run faster, see further, or are otherwise more able to avoid predators or find scarce food, are the ones who are more likely to survive and produce offspring. Those offspring are themselves more likely to survive because they will tend to inherit the same qualities which enabled their parents to survive.

Since Darwin's time, it has been shown that these inherited characteristics such as agility and eyesight are passed on to each generation by a particular arrangement or chain of molecules, called DNA, which is present in each cell of every creature's body. The reason why parents and offspring resemble each other is that similar arrangements of these molecules are found in each generation. But sometimes in the copying of the DNA arrangement of molecules onto the next generation, an accidental mistake is made by nature, and this random variation may result in the birth of a member of the species who is more developed in some particular way and who, of course, passes on that advantage to his offspring. So evolution proceeds.

But in addition to physical characteristics, instincts are inherited from parents. Thus, a well-fed kitten will torment and kill a mouse. Yes, objectively it's cruel, but subjectively the kitten has been programmed to behave in this instinctual way by the DNA molecules it inherited from its parents. Similarly, male animals will instinctively engage in contests with each other for the attention of the females. The stronger wins the fight, and so fathers the young who will be strong like their father. It is noticeable that most instincts are selfish in that they promote self-interest.

Humans, too have inherited instincts. We, according to Darwin, are descended from the earliest forms of life, and all creatures ever since have been competing for food and mates. We see the competitiveness surviving today. The most obvious example is the aggression that leads to wars, but other examples are the obsessive desire to win at sport, aiming to be top in exams, seeking promotion at work and competing for a member of the opposite sex. All are for selfish advantage, and are the relic of millennia of similar activity so inherited and motivated.

So perhaps the author of the Adam and Eve story was pictorially describing a truth that the propensity to sin comes from within us. For, although, historically false, the story seems spiritually accurate. And perhaps it is right to speak of original sin, since it's been passed down the generations with the DNA molecules (the genes) from the earliest times. The current high crime rates have been attributed to poverty, bad housing, poor educational and leisure facilities and the like. But however much such social factors are improved, crime and unkind behaviour will persist, because their source lies not outside but within us.

St. Paul describes this inner difficulty to resist temptation, even when we really want to do the good thing. He says, "I do not understand my own actions. For I do not do what I want, but I do the very thing I hate. I can will what is right but I cannot do it. For I do not do the good I want, but the evil I do not want is what I do. Now if I do what I do not want, it is no longer I that do it, but sin which dwells within me." (Romans 7:18–20).

Should Christians Be Vegetarian?

For guidance a Christian naturally turns to the Bible. There one finds that animal sacrifice was one of the main elements in Israelite Temple worship. Originally, all slaughter of animals, even for domestic consumption, was performed at a sanctuary and was considered a sacred act. However, after Josiah's centralisation of worship in Jerusalem and the destruction of the other sanctuaries (620 BCE) slaughter for domestic consumption was allowed elsewhere. A sacrificial animal was slaughtered in the Temple, and, in many cases, after the sacred parts had been offered to God and after the priest had taken his allotted portion, the remainder of the meat was eaten by the offeror of the sacrifice and his family.

We learn from Genesis that it was believed that man was originally not a meat-eater, for we are told that God gave him for food, every plant yielding seed and every tree with seed in its fruit. And to every beast, bird and creeping thing he gave every green plant, meaning presumably the leaves. This herbivorous system was viewed in the age of the prophets as the idyllic state which would prevail in God's Kingdom. In Isaiah 11, we read, "The wolf shall dwell with the lamb, and the leopard shall lie down with the kid, and the calf and the lion and the fatling together, and a little child shall lead them."(11:6–9).

But after the flood, in Genesis 9 God is reported to have given fresh directions to Noah and his sons, "Every moving thing that lives shall be food for you, and as I gave you the green plants, I give you everything." He adds the requirement of shechitah, "Only you shall not eat flesh with its life, that is, its blood." All the blood must be drained out of meat and this provision is the foundation of the kosher regulations which are still observed by orthodox Jews today. But the kosher requirement does not protect the life of the animal. Admittedly, it is prohibited to eat some animals, fishes, birds and creeping things (Leviticus 11), but here again the prohibitions seem to be motivated not so much by concern for the lives of the prohibited creatures as by concern as to which animals were fit for sacrifice. They had to conform to the Israelite concept of what a creature should resemble, an animal must be cloven footed and chew the cud, a fish should have fins and scales.

This freedom to eat any moving thing seems to accord to the predatory system which governs nature 'red in tooth and claw'. For under that system many species of animals, fishes, birds and insects survive by killing and eating other smaller creatures which in turn subsist by killing and eating still smaller creatures. The predatory system is indeed a difficulty in theism. Because Jesus and the prophets of Israel revealed to us a God who is loving and merciful, the predatory system under which many creatures live seems a strange evolutionary mechanism for such a loving God to have chosen.

This system presumably has the consequence that many animals live in a state of fear during much of their lives. So, the question arises, 'Why could not all creatures have been herbivores, plant eaters?' This assumes that God guided the evolution of creation including animals, whereas if He created the chemicals and atmosphere necessary for the Big Bang, and then left nature to evolve, He would not be responsible for the predatory system. However, in raising this question, we are cautioned by Isaiah, "Shall the axe vaunt itself over him who hews with it, or the saw magnify itself against him who wields it? (10:15), for we, as finite humans, can have little comprehension of the concerns of the infinite. When we turn to Jesus' possible views, assessment is also difficult. He was a man of his time and culture, and animal rights and welfare were apparently not current issues in the minds of his contemporaries. He did not campaign against animal sacrifice in the Temple and he partook of the lamb in the Passover meal. Presumably he ate kosher meat and fish as part of his diet. He told the parable of the Prodigal Son where the fatted calf was killed for the feast upon the son's return. Fish were eaten in the feedings of the 5,000 and 4,000.

So in trying to assess what Jesus' attitude towards the slaughter of animals for food would have been in this generation, we can only speculate as to how the ethical standards which he did enunciate, can be applied to animals. The command to love our neighbours in the sense of seeking their welfare can reasonably be applied to animals. Jesus believed that his Father so cared for his creation that not one sparrow would fall to the ground without his Father's will. (Matthew 10:29) We should therefore not do anything which would needlessly cause his creatures pain. Man can live without meat, indeed without fish or fowl.

If, however, animals were not killed and sold for food, there would be no incentive for farmers to breed and nurture them, and so fewer animals would be born and lives created. And it's surely a good thing that new animals should be borne provided they are to live contented lives, even if they are to be ended before their natural duration. But it's doubtful whether some creatures do live contented lives. Some chicken are reared in batteries, and some lambs and calves are kept and transported in cramped conditions. Some cows suffer from feet and leg conditions because their udders are allowed to accumulate too much milk. Perhaps Christian efforts in this area should be directed to protesting against the unkind treatment which creatures bred for ultimate slaughter suffer in their abbreviated lives.

As man is an agent in bringing into existence animal lives for his food, loving our neighbour surely entails that he allows nothing to jeopardise their welfare. For, through the farmer, modern man too is a predator just as were his primitive forbears with club and, later, bow and arrow. If the ideal in Genesis 1 and Isaiah 11 is the abolition of the predator system so that, 'the wolf shall dwell with the lamb', it behoves man, ideally, to cease to kill or at least to be vigilant for the welfare of his prey.

"Is It Lawful for a Man to Divorce His Wife?" (Mark 10:2)

This was the question which, according to Mark's report, the Pharisee asked Jesus in order to 'test' him. The prophet Malachi had in the 5th century BCE expressed God's hate of divorce (2:16). The extent of a man's right to divorce his wife was a controversial issue in the time of Jesus. This was due to different interpretations of the relevant provision of the laws of Moses, for the laws of Moses, as interpreted by the Rabbis, governed, for the Jew, every action and circumstance in his daily life. The relevant provision was Deuteronomy 24:1 which assumes that a man may divorce his wife if she "finds no favour in his eyes because he has found some indecency in her." Amongst the Pharisees, there were two schools of thought as to what constituted "indecency" in this context. According to the Mishnah the followers of the Jewish scholar, Shammai, considered that only adultery constituted 'indecency', whereas the followers of his rival, Hillel, interpreted 'indecency' as including almost any complaint, e.g. that the wife had spoiled a meal (Gittin 9:10).

So in reply to Jesus' counter question as to what Moses commanded, the Pharisees correctly replied that Moses permitted a man to divorce his wife by a note of dismissal (appropriately called a 'git' in Hebrew). This was simply handed to the wife, no court proceedings were involved. Jesus then makes a fascinating distinction between the Biblical laws. Jesus was generally observant and supportive of the Mosaic laws in the Pentateuch, because, like other Jews, he believed them to be God-given. He only differed with the Pharisees over how they should be interpreted, the definition of work on the Sabbath being a good example. Yet Jesus says here that the law permitting divorce was only given by Moses as a concession because of their hardness of heart. God's law based in creation supersedes this Mosaic concession. He quotes from Genesis that God made humans male and female (I:27; 5:2) and that for this reason a man should leave his father and mother, and be joined to a wife and the two shall become one flesh. "What, therefore, God has joined together, let not man put asunder." (Mark 10:9)

Jesus thus condemned divorce on the ground that God had declared that a man and his wife became one flesh. He argues that sexual intercourse results in one flesh and creates the obligation of permanent union. This argument presumably involves the condemnation of any sexual intercourse unless the couple intends it to be the start of a permanent union, in the sense of marriage, whether formally solemnised or not. For the Hebrew 'ishto' at Genesis (2:24) translated 'his wife' would include 'his woman' as would Mark's Greek 'gunaika autou' at 10:7. If unmarried persons have sexual congress, they too become physiologically 'one flesh' from that moment. This conclusion accords with the law at Exodus 22:16–17 where if a man seduces an unbetrothed virgin, he must marry her. (cf. Deuteronomy 22:28).

Jesus' teachings on divorce were absolute for when questioned further indoors by the disciples, he says "Whoever divorces his wife and marries another commits adultery against her" (Mark 10:11). Matthew, perhaps influenced by the public opinion of his day (writing about 90 CE) makes an exception in the case of the wife's adultery (19:9). Surprisingly, he adds that if she divorces her husband and marries another, she commits adultery, since in Jewish law the wife could not divorce the husband by serving a 'git' on him. Later, and perhaps in Jesus' day she could ask the scribes for an order requiring her husband to serve a 'git' upon her. Perhaps Mark inserted this sentence about the wife divorcing for the benefit of Gentile readers since in Roman law the wife could divorce.

Jesus' teaching on divorce is well attested in the Gospels and is doubtless authentic. Paul writes with the authority of Jesus at 1 Corinthians 7:10–11, "To the married I give charge, not I but the Lord, that the wife should not separate from her husband (but if she does let her remain single or else be reconciled to her husband) and that the husband should not divorce his wife."

Although Jesus thus believed God's will to be that marriage should be permanent, and that the sexual joining of any man and woman produced an indissoluble union, is it possible that in his absolute prohibition of divorce he was mistaken concerning his Father's will? Clearly the answer to this question will be affected by an assessment of Jesus' relationship to the Godhead. But it is perhaps arguable that the God of love revealed by Jesus would not wish a man and wife to remain together in circumstances where intentionally or unintentionally the couple were causing each other or their children continual misery. Certain cases of unsoundness of mind might produce a similar moral justification for divorce. Admittedly, in such situations the 'one flesh' could be preserved by the couple separating and not remarrying, but again it seems unmerciful to impose on a person lifelong celibacy because of an unfortunate choice of a partner. Perhaps, instead of the rigid alternatives of celibacy or permanently unhappy cohabitation in a first and only marriage, Jesus' followers should rather apply the golden rule of 'loving our neighbour as our self' (Leviticus 19:18; cf. Matthew 5:43).Since a spouse is the closest neighbour, the golden rule would require the doing in marital matters of whatever is most conducive to the welfare of the other party to the marriage. This might include divorce.

Reliance on the golden rule may however, be only a convenient escape route from the difficulty of Jesus' specific prohibition. That prohibition should certainly be the ideal which, like the other ethics of the Sermon on the Mount, his followers should strain to follow.

Can There Be a Just War Even Though Intentional Killing Is Necessarily Involved?

A war could presumably be a just and holy war if it was authorised by God. In the Hebrew Scriptures, there are several instances where God is reported to have commanded the Israelites to fight tribes who resisted Israel's conquest of the Promised Land. Thus Yahweh told Saul, through Samuel, to attack the Amalekites and destroy them together with their livestock for this very reason. And when Saul didn't destroy King Agag and the cattle and sheep, Saul was rejected as king by Yahweh (1 Samuel 15). But surely this was not a holy war nor a just war—Samuel the Prophet must have been mistaken in thinking that God was instructing him in this way. So can there be a just war? As Christians we look firstly to Jesus for guidance. In the Sermon on the Mount, we read his teaching of non-resistance, of turning the other cheek, of loving our enemies, of praying for those who persecute us. Judged by this criterion, it seems that war can never be just or holy or according to God's will. Admittedly, Jesus may have been exaggerating in order to impress on his hearers the duty to accept injury and attempt reconciliation, for he said, "Blessed are the peacemakers, for they shall be called sons of God" (Matthew 15:9). However the non-resistance of which Jesus speaks probably relates to personal enemies. Jesus refers to the sixth commandment of the Decalogue, "Thou shalt not kill" (Exodus 20:13). The Hebrew verb there for 'kill' is 'razah' which is only used in the Scriptures for killing a personal enemy, not killing in war. Moreover, judicial execution was positively required by the law given to Moses on Sinai. Stoning to death was the penalty for serving other gods, and even for work such as gathering firewood on the Sabbath (Numbers 15:35). And as mentioned, God was believed to have commanded the slaughter of some enemies of Israel.

So in the Sermon on the Mount Jesus does not speak directly about killing in war. Yet elsewhere he seems to have supported retributive justice i.e. the punishment of wickedness. In Matthew 23, he foretells a dire fate for Jerusalem for killing the prophets and in the parable of the

Grand Assize (25), he describes the plight of the wicked at the Last Judgment. In the Marcan Apocalypse (13) he prophesies the tribulation attending the Last Days. In this teaching, however, Jesus is prophesying a future punishment by God of evil mankind, not a slaughter by one man of another. And it is noteworthy that Jesus continually rejected the temptation to become a warlike Messiah like King David. There are sayings of Jesus on personal violence from which inferences might be drawn concerning his attitude to war but they appear to be inconsistent. (see Matthew 26, 52-53) St. Augustine in the 4th century considered conditions for just war but it was St. Thomas Aquinas in the 13th century who formulated the requirement for a just war and the conduct which was permissible for a Christian. However, the defensive war required no special moral justification. It was an involuntary act forced upon a peaceful community which need not justify its response. But taking up arms as the aggressor required special moral justification. To such offensive war they applied their conditions for a just war. The problem was the difficulty in the reconciliation of the love of peace with the voluntary procurement of death and destruction.

The modern Christian view of the just war has been expressed to incorporate the following requirements:

The amount of force must not be more than is strictly necessary.

The evils which the war creates must not be greater than the evils which it is designed to correct. (The difficulty here is that the comparison can be made with discernment only after the war has been started, cf. the recent situation in Iraq.)

Force must be discriminatory and must not be aimed at innocent persons who are not combatants or directly engaged in the war effort.

The war must be defensive in character.

The aim of the war must be to re-establish creative and friendly relations with the enemy as soon as he has come to his right mind (What is the right mind of the defeated enemy is presumably determined by the victor!).

There is clearly tension between man-made theories of a just war and Jesus teaching of non-resistance. Even if that teaching related only to conflict between individuals, Jesus might as well have applied the same spirit to conflict between nations. Nevertheless, if it has to be accepted that fallen mankind will make wars, the concept of a just war and the conditions attaching to it may tend to limit the barbarism involved. The source of the modern concept may be seen in the humanitarian teaching of Jesus.

The New Covenant

The title page or frontispiece to the RSV version of the New Testament states, "The New Covenant commonly called The New Testament." To discover the reason for this title, 'The New Covenant' we must look at the history of the Hebrews.

About 1300 BCE on Mt. Sinai (otherwise called Horeb) God, according to the Book of Exodus (19:20) agreed to be the God of Israel, and the Israelites promised to obey God's laws. To make the agreement or covenant binding on the parties, it was customary, following the practice in making treaties between tribes, for animals to be sacrificed and for their blood to be thrown on the parties to the covenant. On Mt Sinai, half of the blood was thrown on the altar which represented God.

It may have been thought that when Jerusalem was sacked by the Babylonians in 586 BCE, the Sinai covenant was rendered obsolete. For about that time Jeremiah prophesied that the Lord would make a new covenant with Israel, not written on tablets of stone like the old covenant but metaphorically written in their hearts (31:33). Yahweh, on his part, would be their God and they would be his people and keep his laws. Nobody would need to teach anybody else about the Lord for they would all have direct access to God. A new covenant was possible despite Israel's breaches of the old one because God would remove the barrier created by Israel's sins.

But people sometimes say, "What is the relevance of the Old Testament to Jesus and Christianity, and therefore to us?" The relevance is that Jesus, being an observant Jew, knew intimately the Hebrew Scriptures (Old Testament), and was guided by them in deciding his own rôle and relationship to his heavenly Father. He probably saw himself as fulfilling prophesies about the Suffering Servant of Isaiah (53) and the

Son of man mentioned in Daniel 7. His thinking was permeated by the Hebrew Scriptures, which he often quoted, and he probably also saw himself as the arranger and mediator of that new covenant between God and man which Jeremiah had prophesied.

For at the Last Supper, according to Paul in 1 Corinthians (11:25), Jesus took the cup and said, "This cup is the new covenant sealed by my blood." Mark has, "This is my blood of the covenant, shed for many." (14:24). Thus it appears that Jesus took from the Exodus story of the old Covenant on Sinai the requirement that a covenant between God and man had to be sealed by a sacrifice and the shedding of blood. The difference from the old covenant was that the blood was to be human, his own shed on the cross.

There are differing views as to what Jesus meant by his other words and actions over the bread and wine at the Last Supper. I think he was telling his disciples in a dramatic way how and why He was going to die. He was saying, 'My body will be broken for you like this bread I'm breaking. My blood will be poured out for you, like this wine I'm pouring out. The idea that he was commanding the disciples to eat the bread as if it was His body, and to drink the wine as if it was His blood, is surely mistaken. As discussed above, Jesus and his disciples were observant Jews, and the suggestion that the bread should be eaten as if his body, and the wine drunk as if his blood, would be abhorrent to them. In the Law of Moses it is stated, "For the life of every creature is the blood of it; therefore I have said to the people of Israel, 'You shall not eat the blood of any creature, for the life of every creature is its blood; whoever eats it shall be cut off.' (Leviticus 17:14).

So I prefer Paul's report of Jesus' words and actions in which while breaking the bread he said, "This is my body which is broken for you". Similarly, the words over the wine were spoken before giving the cup to the disciples, so avoiding the idea that He was asking the bread and wine to be consumed as His body and blood. The words were spoken while breaking the bread and pouring the wine. However, in Mark's account the words 'Take, eat: this is my body ' were spoken while giving the bread, and it is this instruction to eat the bread as his body and the wine as his blood, which gave rise to the Romish doctrine of Transubstantiation, the

conversion of the bread and wine into Christ's body and blood
.

As mentioned above, I prefer Paul's report of the Last Supper and think that at the Last Supper Jesus was declaring to the disciples by his words and action over the bread and wine that he was to die for them and that his blood would seal and sanctify the New Covenant. Was the New Covenant instituted by Jesus the New Covenant prophesied by Jeremiah? An important part of Jeremiah's covenant is that God will put His law within them by writing it on their hearts, and the law in Jesus' covenant is the law of Moses as interpreted in the teaching of Jesus in the Sermon on the Mount and elsewhere. Jesus similarly said, "The Kingdom of heaven is within you," as our acceptance of Jesus' teaching allows his Father's kingship to rule in our hearts. Thus it appears that Jesus' new covenant fulfilled the prophesy of Jeremiah.

Apart from the Resurrection, that New Covenant was the culmination of Jesus' work on earth and surely justifies calling the New Testament the New Covenant.

Chapter 5
Liberal Ecumenism (and Beyond?)

Two Branches of One Faith?

The relationship between Christianity and Judaism should, from the Christian standpoint, reflect to some extent the relationship between Jesus and Judaism, although allowance has to be made for the differences between the Judaism(s) of his day and of today. That relationship can be summarised in the statement that Jesus was an observant Jew. But, if so, why was he crucified? Because, many would say, the Jewish Sanhedrin (dominated by the high priests and other Sadducees) saw Jesus as a threat to the continuation of their limited powers to govern their countrymen. They feared that if Jesus continued to 'stir up the people', the Roman 'praefectus' (Pilate) would anticipate a Jewish uprising and would remove from the Sanhedrin the powers which Rome had delegated to it.

Yet, after Jesus' death, his first followers remained observant Jews, attending Temple and synagogue. They seem to have been considered a separate group or a sect within Judaism. Luke reports in Acts (5:38–9) that the honoured Pharisee, Gamaliel, declared in the Sanhedrin, "…if this plan or this undertaking is of God you will not be able to overthrow them. You might even be found opposing God!" And at Acts (24:5) Paul's accuser, Tertullus, describes him as "a ringleader of the sect of the Nazarenes".

In Palestine the separation from Judaism took place between 90 CE, when the curse on the heretics and Nazarenes was inserted in the daily prayer, the Eighteen Benedictions, and 135 CE, when the Christians refused to support the rebellion on behalf of Bar Kokhba, the alleged Messiah. The gradual alienation of the Christians is unlikely to have been caused by the Jewish failure to recognise Jesus as Messiah, since there were several other Messianic claimants in addition to Jesus and BarKokhbar, and it was not an offence in Jewish law to make such a claim. A more probable cause was the increasing Jewish awareness of the spread of Christianity amongst the Gentiles who worshipped Jesus as God, and did not observe the Jewish law. Although there were two main kinds of Palestinian Jewish Christians, the Ebionites and the Nazarenes, neither kind worshipped Jesus as God.

From the Jewish standpoint, Christian non-observance of the dietary and other cultic laws of Moses was justified since those laws were addressed only to the Israelites and alien residents with them, the 'gerim' in Hebrew. The 'gerim' were obliged to observe the Mosaic laws (including the kosher requirement to drain the blood) but were exempted from the laws on cultic purity, prohibited meat (e.g. pig) and the Passover. But even if Gentile Christians are not physically resident in Israel, are they not, as followers of Jesus, the observant Jew, so spiritually close to Judaism as to be equated to the 'gerim' for law-observance?

Another difficulty from the Christian standpoint over law-observance is that, according to Luke, the Jewish Christian leaders decided at the Council of Jerusalem in CE 49 that Gentile Christians should abstain from 'what is strangled and from blood', i.e. they should observe the kosher laws. This is however, a matter for internal Christian debate, since the Jews consider that Gentiles are only liable to observe the Noahide laws which were mainly of an ethical nature.

What persists as the principal obstacle to closer religious association between Jews and Christians is the status of Jesus. To the Jews, whose fundamental belief is in the unicity of God as witnessed in the Shema (Deuteronomy 6:6), the Christian doctrine of the Trinity appears as tritheism (the worship of three Gods) and, consequently, idolatry. Nevertheless, since such amicable progress has been made by Jews and Trinitarian Christians in recent times, one might reasonably expect that there would be even greater prospects of reconciliation between liberal Jews and liberal Christians particularly as the latter include some holding a Unitarian belief.

Mark reports (7:24) that Jesus healed a Gentile woman at Tyre where he sought to be alone. Vincent Taylor suggested that Jesus sought privacy because he wished to meditate. Certainly it is almost immediately after this that Mark reports at 8:31, Jesus' warning at Caesarea Philippi that it will be necessary for him to suffer at the hands of men (cf. 9:31; 10:33–4). This is the basis of Schweitzer's claim that the result of Jesus' reassessment over the failure of both the Woes and the Kingdom to materialise, was that he became convinced that he himself would have to undergo the suffering—in place of men generally—in order to satisfy Satan's demands for justice, and thus enable His Father to bring in the kingdom.

It is after this teaching at Caesarea Philippi about his suffering that Jesus begins his long journey south through Galilee to Jerusalem. He may well have anticipated that the Passover at Jerusalem to which he was travelling, would be the most probable occasion for his suffering and death. For in Jerusalem was the Temple, the power base of the chief priests, scribes and elders, those who formed the Sanhedrin, to which Rome delegated self-government in most internal Jewish affairs. It was obvious that Rome would remove that power and prestige from the Jewish establishment if a charismatic Galilean preacher, whom the crowd saw as a Messiah likely to free them from Roman tyranny, continued his teaching about a kingdom not of Tiberius, the Roman Emperor, but of the Jewish God. Whether Jesus had already decided that he would drive out the dealers in currency and animals and thus provoke confrontation with the chief priests, one can only speculate. But there is evidence that he chafed at waiting for his testing-time to commence, "I have a baptism to be baptized with; and how I am constrained until it is accomplished!" (Luke 12:50)

It is to this period when Jesus realised that the arrival of the kingdom would be further postponed until he, himself, had died to bring it in, by satisfying Satan, that the saying in Mark 9:1 should probably be assigned, "There are some standing here who will not taste death until they see the kingdom of God come with power." but only God could predict the exact time of its arrival (Mark 13:32).

However, since Jesus expected the kingdom to arrive on the heels of his own death, the realisation of his betrayal by

Judas convinced him that in a few days there would be early evidence for the belief in the Incarnation, the belief that the one creator God lived on earth as a human being in the person of Jesus. The Letters to the Philippians and to the Colossians were written by Paul (or one of his circle) between 56 and 60 CE. In Philippians 2:26, the author writes about Jesus, "Though he was in the form of God, (he) did not count equality with God, a thing to be grasped, but emptied himself being born in the likeness of men." And in Colossians (1:15). He writes, "He is the image of the invisible God, the first-born of all creation, all things were created through him and for him. For in Him all the fullness of God was pleased to dwell."

Apart from periods of uncertainty or Arianism in the fourth and fifth centuries, this belief in the equality of Jesus with God has dominated Christian orthodoxy and the wording of the creeds recited Sunday by Sunday. In the Nicaean creed, the worshipper declares his belief in Jesus as, "Very God of very God, Begotten, not made, being of one substance with the Father by whom all things were made."

This dogma may be true, if we grant that a Creator has made the world, we must surely grant that He is able to occupy the body of one of His creatures. But a reluctance to accept this dogma should not be allowed to stand as an intellectual obstacle for one who wishes to accept the life, death and teaching of Jesus as the guide of his life.

During his lifetime Jesus was considered by his contemporaries as just another man, although a gifted one, and was treated as such. His own neighbours were surprised by his teachings and asked each other whence he derived his wisdom, "Is not this the carpenter's son? Is not his mother called Mary?", "Where then did this man get all this?" (Matthew 13:54–56). For Jesus displayed the normal human emotions, compassion, joy, sadness and anger.

In the Gospels (apart from John's) he denies that he is God, both explicitly and implicitly.

He treats his Father as a separate, other, person of quite different status. In Mark 13:32, concerning the time of the Day of Judgement, he says, "But of that day or of that hour no one knows, not even the Son, but only the Father." In Mark (10:17) when he is addressed as "Good Teacher", he responds, "Why do you call me good? No one is good but God alone.", and his separation from God is manifest in his tragic cry from the Cross, "My God, my God, why hast thou forsaken me?" His prayers are naturally directed outside himself—to his Father.

He conforms to the Jewish belief in the singularity of God at Mark (12:29). When asked which is the first commandment, he starts his reply by quoting the Jewish Shema, "Hear, O Israel, the Lord our God, the Lord is one." (Deuteronomy 6:4). He implicitly denies his own deity in his teaching of the Lord's Prayer, and in His proclamation of the Kingdom of God which he treats as his Father's, not his own.

The titles which he did apply to himself during his lifetime were 'prophet', 'Christ' and 'Son of man'. When the people of Nazareth rejected his teaching, he commented that a prophet is not without honour, except in his own country (Mark 6:4). And referring to his own death he accepted that it was not fitting that a prophet should die away from Jerusalem (Luke 13:33).

'Christ' is the Greek translation of the Hebrew 'Messiah', meaning 'one anointed/appointed by God to a particular task such as king or high priest'. When Jesus at Caesarea Philippi asked the disciples who people thought he was, Peter replied that he was the Christ (Mark 8:29). The Jews expected a Christ Messiah like King David who would make the Jews the supreme nation. So Jesus was very reserved about accepting this title since His own Messiahship (appointment) was to bring in his Father's Kingdom, not Jewish military supremacy.

Similarly, the description, 'Son of God' had a purely human application. It was used for anyone who was considered to be very close to God, such as Israel itself, and its king; thus God says of David in the Psalms (2:7), "You are my son. Today I have begotten you."

Nearer to Jesus' day, the charismatic Rabbi Hanina ben Dosa was called 'my son' by the voice from heaven—but there is evidence that in Jesus' day the title was used for the expected Messiah—which is not surprising since he would naturally be thought to be close to God. So when at his trial, Jesus answered, "I am" to the High Priest's question, "Are you the Christ, the Son of the Blessed (i.e., God)?" (Mark 14:61–2), he was not asserting any divine rôle. Such was his reserve concerning his Messiahship. Similarly, there are reports that suggest that Jesus replied to the High Priest's question saying, "You say I am (Son of the Blessed)". (Mathew 26:63–69).

But Jesus added to his reply in Mark and Matthew, "and you will see the Son of man sitting at the right hand of Power (i.e. God) and coming down with the clouds of heaven." Jesus here sees himself as the Son of man coming in judgement at the last days as prophesied in Daniel 7. Although, the Son is both there and in the Parables of Enoch placed on a heavenly throne—his distinction from God is thereby accentuated.

It is only in John's Gospel that Jesus is reported to make express claims to divinity. There he says, "Before Abraham was, I am" (John, 8:49) and "I and the Father are one," (John, 10:30). He also says, "He who has seen me, has seen the Father" (John 14:9) and "I am the way, the truth and the life; no one comes to the Father but by me." (John 14:6).

These statements and many others in that Gospel, are such a contrast in their egocentricity to the reserved Jesus of the other Gospels who points always to his Father's kingdom and not to himself, that it is easier to regards much of John's Gospel as the extrapolations of the author based on his meditation on Jesus' briefer utterances in the earlier Gospels.

An implicit claim to Godhead might be seen in Jesus declaring the forgiveness of sins in Mark (2:5) and Luke (7:48). In both cases Jesus says, "Your sins are forgiven". However, the correct translation for Luke should be, "Your sins have been forgiven", because the Greek verb is in the perfect tense (as in his previous verse) while in many manuscripts of the Marcan verse, the perfect tense is also used. The perfect tense means that Jesus is saying, "Your sins have been forgiven" (i.e., by God not by Jesus). An implicit claim to divinity might also be discerned in the 'miracles' of healing. These were probably thought to have a supernatural cause because the psychosomatic effect on the patient's body of his faith in the healer's ability was not then appreciated, as it is in the case of faith healers today.

In short, Jesus himself did not make divine claims, explicit or implicit. After the Cross, although the extended resurrection appearances may show God's seal of approval on Jesus' life, they did not necessarily connote divinity since other deceased persons were reported to have appeared with spiritual bodies before the time of Jesus (e.g. Samuel at 1 Samuel 28:14). After Jesus' death his Jewish followers in Palestine continued to regard him as the Messiah but gave him no divine status. It was Paul and his circle, who preached to the Jews of the Dispersion and to the Gentiles that Jesus was God, as quoted above. This belief was easily accepted by Gentiles of the Roman world who readily ascribed deity to their heroes as mentioned above. At Lystra Paul and Barnabas were worshipped as Gods, having healed a cripple (Acts 14: 10-12 cf. Peter at Acts 3:12).

It is entirely understandable that a Christian man—after reading about Jesus' teachings, healing and self-sacrificial death—should believe him to be more than a highly gifted and virtuous human being. He may, indeed, be justified in worshipping him as God and it would be rash to deny any reasoned assessment of Jesus' status since much of our faith must rest ultimately on mystique and temperament.

However, people who may find themselves intellectually unable to adopt the orthodox view may still recognise that Jesus' teaching could only have been given by someone especially close to God in spirit—someone, indeed, who was able to reveal God's nature and His will as to how we should live.

Inability to accept the doctrine of the Incarnation should, therefore, not deter seekers from following Jesus and joining the fellowship of an inclusive Christian Church.

"In vain do they worship me, teaching as doctrines the precepts of men." (Mark 7:7)

There is some doubt whether Jesus uttered this quotation from Isaiah 29:13, since it is taken from the Septuagint (Greek) translation of the Bible, and Jesus would more likely have quoted from the Hebrew original; the Hebrew text makes the different point that 'their fear of me is a commandment of men learned by rote', i.e. a mechanical lip-service, a memorised ritual. However, "teaching as doctrines the precepts of men" is in Mark's Gospel, so either Jesus or a passer-on of the oral tradition or Mark himself must have levelled the charge that the scribes were teaching in this way. This accusation of teaching man-made rules as if they were laws of God seems a valid one, for it relates to the practice of hand washing before meals which the Pharisees and scribes were urging Jesus and his disciples to follow.

The purpose of this hand washing was not hygiene but the avoidance of cultic impurity passing from hands to food and thence to the eater, thus (inter alia) disqualifying him from entry to the Temple. But there was nothing in the purity laws given by God to Moses at Sinai and recorded in the Hebrew Bible which demanded this washing. It was a ruling of the scribes applying only to a super-pious group called 'haberim', and was not deducible from any provision of the written law—it was a tradition of men. When a scribal ruling could not be deduced from the written law, it was defended as being a law handed down orally by God to Moses at Sinai, but many would consider this to be later rationalisation.

As Mark interpolates, there were many other habits such as bathing on return from market and the ritual washing of pots, etc. that were not required by the written law of Moses. It is this tradition of the elders, rules passed down from scribe to scribe, that Jesus condemns as teaching man-made regulations as if they were the doctrines of God.

"Yet Wisdom Is Justified by All Her Children" Luke (7:35)

This saying of Jesus appears at the end of a passage (7:18–35) which Luke has drawn from the written source, Q, which Matthew also used in his parallel passage (11:2–19). It is Jesus' final comment on a similitude in which he likens the contrasting attitudes of his contemporaries towards John the Baptizer and himself to one set of children in the market place who call to the others (Matthew 11:16) on the lines, 'We thought you might like to dance so we played our pipes for you. You didn't want that, so we wailed for you to weep, but you didn't want that either!'

The point being made is that the Jews of Jesus' day rejected God's messenger in whatever form he came. John the Baptist lived a very ascetic life (Mark 1:6) yet they accused him of having a demon (1:18; as Jesus, Mark 3:22). Jesus, in contrast, enjoyed dining and fellowship, and is accused of being a glutton, a drunkard and a friend of sinners. Just like the children being played dance, music or dirges, the people are never satisfied (Christologically it's noteworthy that Jesus here treats John's ministry as comparable to his own).

Then follows Jesus' apothegm, "Yet wisdom is justified by *all* her children,". Matthew's version of this sentence is, "Yet wisdom is justified by her deeds.", but we think Luke's 'all her children' is a more Jewish expression in this context (some manuscripts of Matthew have 'children' but scribes have probably here harmonised his version with Luke's).

Wisdom teaching had a long and international history in Egypt, Assyria, Israel and elsewhere in the East as instruction for the successful secular life in the family, in business and at the princely court. The special development in Israel is that subsequently, as evidenced by the books of Proverbs and Sirach, wisdom undergoes a theological makeover, and is equated to the wisdom of God as disclosed in Torah (Sirach 21:11). Ultimately, in Christian thinking, wisdom becomes identified with the teaching of Jesus, who himself becomes the wisdom of God (1 Corinthians 1:24)

Another development in Israel was that wisdom was hypostasized (treated as a person). Thus at Proverbs 8:22–31, Wisdom declares that she was the first of God's acts of creation, and that in creation she was at His side like a master worker (or little child, the Hebrew noun is ambiguous). In Proverbs 1 and 8, Wisdom cries out in the squares and cross roads urging the people to attend to her (cf. Sirach 24); at Wisdom of Solomon (10: 1, 2 and 4), it is recounted how Wisdom protected Adam, at the flood, saving the earth by 'steering the righteous man by a paltry piece of wood'. Wisdom also preserved Joseph in Egypt, and led the people through the Red Sea and the wilderness at the Exodus. However, no threat to the unity of God was perceived in these developments since Wisdom was considered either as the agent of God or as an aspect of His nature.

So in Jesus apothegm 'wisdom' deserves a capital letter since 'God in his wisdom' is surely intended. We think the meaning of the sentence to be that God's wisdom is vindicated, i.e. shown to be true wisdom, by the diversity of his human followers. For that diversity, except when it has been oppressed by the majority in the name of orthodoxy, has prevailed amongst the countless legions of those who have been brought to God through Jesus. For some Christians have found a closer walk with God by living in an ascetic way like John the Baptist and (to a lesser extent) like the Puritans of recent times; others, like Jesus, have expressed the joy of their faith in an enjoyment of God's created gifts, food, wine etc.

We think that in this parable and sentence Jesus is again urging inclusivity. We are sometimes tempted to treat those who are seeking to follow Jesus, but in a lifestyle or churchmanship different to our own, as not really being fully paid-up Christians. Jesus would perhaps then reply to us, "No, we are all God's children, and his comprehensive wisdom is shown in the way that He created humankind with many different psyches and temperaments so that He receives man's fealty in a rich variety of ways."

The vice, whether we prefer dance or blues, is to consider our step as the only proper approach to God.

The Purpose of Jesus

"Now after John was arrested," Mark tells us, "Jesus came into Galilee, preaching the good news of God and saying, "The time is fulfilled, and the Kingdom of God has drawn near; repent and trust in the good news." (1:15)

Thus the good news which Jesus preached was that God's Kingdom had drawn near. He spoke both of a reign which God was to impose upon the earth in the Last Days (which had almost arrived), and of God's immediate reign in the hearts of those who sought to live their lives according to His will. Indeed, the central purpose of His ministry was to explain by parable and deed, the nature and proximity of the Kingdom and the qualifications for entry into it, either in the Last Days or there and then.

Indeed, he diverted attention from himself to his Father and his Father's Kingdom. To the woman who blessed the womb that bore him, Jesus replied, "Blessed rather are those who hear the word of God and keep it." (Luke 11:28). And when addressed as 'Good Teacher', he replied, "Why do you call me good? No one is good but God alone." (Mark 10:18).

Jesus' concentration on his Father and his Father's Kingdom makes a surprising contrast with the reported teaching of his followers after his resurrection. The impact of the resurrection experience (of whatever kind it was) so affected the disciples that the emphasis of their preaching was not upon the Kingdom but upon Jesus himself. There was a shift from the message of Jesus to the person of Jesus. C.H. Dodd listed nine examples of apostolic teaching recorded in the Acts of the Apostles and in Paul's Letters; the mighty works of Jesus are extolled in them all, but no specific mention is made of the Kingdom which he came to proclaim. Did the teaching of men replace the intent of Jesus here?

The Status of Jesus

The first followers of Jesus were Jewish, and as faithful monotheists, most of them believed Jesus not to be God, but to be the Messiah promised by God at Deuteronomy 18:18 and anointed (hence the title Christ) by God to bring in the Last Days. Their Jewish descendants, the Ebionites and Nazarenes continued this approach; the latter denied Jesus' pre-existence as God, but called him the Son of God, while the former held him to be a man only.

When Peter, Philip and Paul brought Gentiles (i.e. non-Jews) into the Church, the first rules of faith were statements such as 'Jesus is Lord' ('Lord' translating the Greek word 'kurios' which can simply mean 'Master'). But many Gentiles, reflecting on the teaching, healing, death and resurrection of Jesus, estimated him to be more than human. This is shown in the descending and rising of Jesus described in Paul's Letter to the Philippians (2:5–11 written in about 60 CE), and, more categorically, in the statements in his letter to the Colossians (also written about 60 CE) such as, "For in him all things were created, in heaven and on earth, for in him all the fullness of God was pleased to dwell." (1:19).

The early Church Fathers, inheriting the Platonic zeal for analysis, and pondering over the apparent contradiction of one person being both man and God, prepared creeds defining the divinity of Jesus and declaring the relationship between the divine and the human in him. But from the time of the first

Jewish and Gentile Christians the views of Jesus' followers concerning his status have diverged.

Unfortunately, these divergences were not treated as healthy and acceptable differences of opinion; rather were they battlegrounds dividing Christian from Christian. Jesus simply said, "Follow me," but too many of those who did try to follow were infected with the very intolerance against which Jesus had preached (e.g. Mark 9:38–40). A sad example is the history of Arianism. Arius, a deacon of the church at Alexandria from about 318 CE contended that Christ, the Son, although the highest of all creatures, was still a creature created by God. His watchword was that there was a time when Christ was not, and therefore he was subordinate to God. He had many bishops among his supporters but so did his principal opponent, Athanasius, leader of the 'very God of very God', i.e. Trinitarian persuasion. The dispute caused such a stir that the Roman Emperor Constantine summoned a Council of the church at Nicaea in 325 CE. After much discussion, and the operation of the Emperor's influence, the views of Arius were condemned by a majority of two hundred eighteen to two, and he was banished. But even that majority was unhappy with the application to Jesus of the Greek term 'homoousios' (of the same essence as God the Father), and with other phrases not sanctioned by Scripture.

However, when Constantius became Emperor in 350 he convened Church Councils in 353 and 355 specifically to condemn Athanasius, the strict Trinitarian, who only escaped death by fleeing into the desert. Moreover, at the Council of Sirmium, in 357 CE the bishops agreed upon another creed suggesting that the Son is not really God, and declaring the inferiority of the Son and other created things. But the wind of change blew again, and at the Council of Constantinople in 381 CE the Nicaean creed was restored as the standard of orthodoxy and the equal Godhead of Father, Son and Holy Spirit was affirmed. From this time the Trinitarian view of God as three persons of one substance triumphed as the orthodox, dominant, view so that the Church was able to exclude those followers of Jesus whose conscience would not permit them publicly to recite that creed. In fairness, the Arians were equally absolutist when their views held sway; Athanasius was banished three times! But orthodoxy only means the view of the majority and, as we have seen, the majority view changed with the change of Emperor, so that on such a mystery as the Godhead the confidence of a majority should not have involved the exclusion of a minority from common worship and fellowship. However, the majority—clothed in orthodoxy—writes most of the history which controls most of the present, so that many worshippers in mainstream pews today probably consider anything varying from Trinitarianism to be perverse, if not eccentric.

Let me stress here that the mainstream view of the divine nature of Christ may well be correct, and its formulators may have been inspired by the power of God (the Holy Spirit). I am not preaching an Arian, Trinitarian or any other view of the Godhead. I would only suggest to the dogmatist that the nature and composition of the Godhead is a mystery which may be beyond the finite capacity of humankind to comprehend. Whatever our private conviction, we may have to agree with Job, "Therefore I have uttered what I did not understand, things too wonderful for me which I did not know." (42:3).

I have ventured into this Christology in order to submit that the main concern of the first followers and of the Church Fathers was not the pursuit of Jesus' own purpose, the proclamation of the Kingdom, so much as the proclamation of the person of Jesus and the elucidation of His status.

For, in contrast to the proclamation of the early church, Jesus did not claim any superhuman status for himself except in St. John's Gospel. There he says, "Before Abraham was, I am." (8:58) and "I and the Father are one" (10:30). But most scholars would treat that Gospel in the main as the author's meditations upon the Synoptic Gospels. For, indeed, in those other Gospels Jesus expresses a distinction between himself and the Father, both in the sayings quoted earlier, and in the Lord's Prayer and in the declaration that only the Father, not the angels not the Son knows the time of commencement of the Last Days (Mark 13:3).

The high Pauline assessment in Philippians and Colossians may be correct notwithstanding the Synoptic Gospels; alternatively the monotheistic view of Judaism and Islam, treating Jesus simply as a great prophet, may be true, and there is a variety of views between these poles. For

81

example, I think many would agree that Jesus revealed God to man in a very special way.

What seems important is that doctrines on the status of Jesus or kindred matters, unless supported by clear evidence from his teaching, should not be allowed to cause division between Christians or the denial of the title of Christian to any who are trying to follow him.

Doctrines barely supported by Scripture may nevertheless be inspired by God's force (the Holy Spirit); but if they are not, we may, like the scribes, be 'teaching as doctrines the precepts of men'.

The principal argument opposing a belief in God's continued activity in the world is that, although He is traditionally a God of absolute power and love, He does not suspend the laws of nature each time so as to prevent 'natural evil' (evil not caused by man).Thus He does not always suspend the laws of physics to prevent the fires under the earth from producing volcanoes, nor does he suspend the laws of biology to prevent bodily cells coagulating and becoming cancerous. I say 'not always' because I suppose we do not know that He never suspends those laws, although judging by the suffering involved in the unprevented tragedies, it seems that for reasons unknown, He may never suspend those laws. We may think there are occasions when He does so, but we may not appreciate the laws of nature which are operating there. Similarly, in former times some unusual events were classed as supernatural 'acts of God' which later scientific discoveries have shown to accord with the laws of nature.

Upon our evaluation of the above arguments for and against God's willingness to override the natural laws established at creation, may depend our acceptance or rejection of the prophecies of the Day of the Lord and of the arrival of that Kingdom which would break so dramatically upon the physical world. Jesus had prophesied that he would return very soon to inaugurate that Kingdom as Son of Man and Judge, but his prophecy has not been fulfilled.

In contrast, scientists expect the present world to end when the universe, having expanded to the ultimate, shrinks and finally sinks into the 'Black Hole'. That termination would be governed by the laws of physics as established at creation.

On the evaluation of these factors also depends the purpose of our prayers .If God does not intervene in the physical world, then instead of asking God to check a cancerous growth or stem floods, we should ask Him to give strength and comfort to those who are suffering the ordeal; again, rather than praying that God arrest a conflict in the Middle East or elsewhere, we should ask Him to instil in the minds of the leaders of both sides a determination to produce peace.

The attempt to understand the extent of God's involvement in the world is difficult because as Emmanuel Kant explained, "Our brains are so constructed that we are forced to analyse events according to our concepts of time ('then and now'), space ('there and here') and causality ('this moved–that must have caused it')." Perhaps the conceptual spectacles we wear, obscure from us the reality of God's activity in the world, for "my thoughts are not your thoughts, neither are your ways my ways, says the Lord." (Isaiah 55:8)

Islam in Relation to Christianity

It is tragic that both historically and in the present day Islam and Christianity are in conflict. Yet theologically the two faiths have much in common. We will compare very briefly some cardinal tenets of the two faiths.

Muslims and Christians all worship one Supreme Being who in English is called God, and in Arabic, Allah. It seems reasonable to identify God and Allah as the same Supreme Being since in the Qur'an Allah is described as possessing many of the same qualities as the God (Yahweh) of the Hebrew Scriptures. Both are creators of the universe, sovereign, omnipotent and just, yet merciful. The two faiths have the same patriarchal pedigree of Adam, Abraham, Moses, the prophets, and Jesus.

Thus, the Qur'an does not claim that Muhammad founded a new religion, but rather that God revealed his will to Moses and the Hebrew prophets and later to Jesus, and finally to Muhammad (570–632 CE). However, Muslims believe that the Hebrew Scriptures and the Gospels were corrupted by later writers. They believe that after the deaths of the prophets the Jews distorted their mission to witness to the world into a doctrine of divine election as a chosen people. The Qur'an teaches that a similar distortion occurred in Christianity—that God sent Jesus as a prophet yet his message was soon altered by making him into a God—

"The Christians say the Messiah is the Son of God. How they are perverted. They were commanded to serve but one God; there is no God but Him" (9:3) and "Behold, Allah said: 'O Jesus! I will take thee and raise thee to myself and clear thee (of the falsehoods) of those who blaspheme.'" (3:6).

Yet the Muslims honour Jesus as a prophet. Indeed, the Qur'an accepts, and comments positively upon, several Biblical persons and events such as Adam, Noah and the Flood, Abraham and the near-sacrifice of his son Ishmael (not Isaac), and the signs that Moses gave to Pharaoh. Aspects of the nativity of Jesus and John the Baptist are described in detail (3:4 and 5). The Qur'an does not claim to nullify but rather to correct the versions of Scriptures preserved by the Jewish and Christian communities—"People of the Book—Jews and Christians, now there has come to you Our messenger making clear to you many things you have concealed in the Book and effacing many things." (5:15)

A different status is assigned to the words of the Qur'an from that assigned to the words of the Bible. Modern Biblical criticism acknowledges the part played by human authors and editors in the composition and final wording of the Bible.. This is not the case with the Qur'an where the Arabic words are considered to be the actual speech of Allah. Muhammad was only the channel of those words.

However, the most important theological difference between Islam (also Judaism) and Christianity concerns the Qur'an's emphasis on the unicity (taw-hid) of Allah—"They do blaspheme who say: Allah is one of three in a Trinity: for there is no God except one God." (5:10). Five times a day when Muslims worship they declare Islam's radical monotheism, "I witness that there is no God but the God (Allah) and Muhammad is his Messenger." At Surah 5:6 Jesus denies that he told men to worship him and his mother.

The Qur'an condemns associating anything with God or allowing anything to usurp God's place,. as the greatest sin (shirk), saying "God forgives not that aught should be associated with Him. Whosoever associates anything with

God has indeed forged a mighty sin." (22:4). This led to a ban on any image or representation of God or even of Muhammad. Judaism holds this same insistence on the oneness of God as a central belief—"Hear, O Israel: The Lord, our God, is one Lord;" (Deuteronomy 6:4). and the second Commandment forbids any graven image.

This emphasis of Islam and Judaism stands in stark contrast to the mainstream Christian concept of God as three persons of one substance (the Trinity). It also conflicts with the Christian doctrine of the Incarnation—that God took the bodily form of Jesus.

Naturally the unicity of Islam prevented any divinity being accorded to Muhammad and he is not believed to have worked any redemption or atonement for the sins of mankind. Similarly, according to the Qur'an pleas of intercession can be made only to Allah although tradition includes Muhammad.

The attitude towards enemies may constitute a theoretical difference between Islam and Christianity. Jesus exhorted his disciples to love their enemies, turn the other cheek and pray for those who persecuted them.

This teaching has not been observed by all his followers as the medieval Crusades illustrate. Islam contains the doctrine of jihad which means striving against the temptations of self and evil (the greater jihad), and against non-believers (the lesser jihad) . In Muhammad's early years as a prophet he was much engaged in defensive tribal warfare against the Makkas, but the Qur'an does contain teaching such as "Whosoever fights in the way of God and is slain or conquered we shall bring him a mighty wage." (4:10), and "Fight those who believe not in Allah... until they pay the jizyah with willing submission, and feel themselves subdued" (9:4). Contrast "Let there be no compulsion in religion" (2:34).

There have been many different interpretations of verses such as these by Islamic jurists but the majority insist that only a defensive jihad or violence is justified by the Qur'an. Islam becomes involved in military affairs when sharia law comprising the Qur'an. the Hadith and Sunnah governs a country through a Caliph.

Perhaps the most important theme common to Islam and Christianity (and Judaism) is that of the Kingdom of God reigning in people's hearts, Jesus said., "The Kingdom of God is not coming with signs to be observed; nor will they say. 'Lo, here it is! ' or 'There' for behold, the Kingdom of God is within you." (Luke 17:20–21).

The idea had been present in Israel from the seventh century BCE for Jeremiah had prophesied at 31:33: "But this is the covenant which I will make with the house of Israel after those days, says the Lord: I will put my law within them and I will write it upon their hearts in." This concept of God's Kingdom ruling in a person's heart when he observes God's will is also present in Islam for the word 'Islam' means 'submission to the will of God'. The Qur'an reads "Abraham bowed his will to Allah's which is Islam.." (3:67). The will of God is contained, Muslims believe, in the Qur'an and in the Hadith (the thousands of traditions handed down as to what Muhammad said and did and the things he permitted or prohibited— "Say : If you do love Allah, follow me." (3:4). These traditions range from ablutions before prayers and dietary restrictions to beginning with the right foot when putting on shoes. In Judaism the Pentateuch and the Talmud contain similar detailed rules covering sacrifices, inheritance and property rights (e.g. Leviticus 15). The difference in emphasis between the Kingdom of God described by Jesus and the Kingdom in Islam and Judaism may be that in Islam and Judaism God's will is revealed to a greater extent in detailed regulation of behaviour. In Christianity there is greater emphasis on a free spirit of behaviour springing from love of God and neighbour. Love of God and neighbour are, of course, fervently demanded in Islam and Judaism, but may be more demonstrated in the observance of legal rules.

What may these comparisons with Islam suggest to us as Christians? Perhaps they should remind us that God has revealed Himself through many different prophets and holy books and in many other ways. Therefore, despite the hostilities of Muslim extremists, and mindful of historical Christian cruelties, we should acknowledge, that just as we believe that God revealed Himself through the Hebrew prophets and Jesus, so He also revealed Himself through the Qur'an. "The Believers are but a single Brotherhood: so make peace and reconciliation." (Sura 49:1).

Chapter 6
Liberal Miscellanea

"Who are you?" (John 1:19) — the significance of John the Baptist

Mark describes the function of the Baptist succinctly—he preached "a baptism of repentance for the forgiveness of sins" (Mark 1:4; Luke 3:3). Josephus, the Jewish historian who lived in Rome, wrote in about CE 90 that John "was a good man and had exhorted the Jews to live righteous lives, to practise justice towards their fellows and piety towards God, and so doing to join in baptism. In his view this was a necessary preliminary if baptism was to be acceptable to God. They must not employ it to gain pardon for whatever sins they committed, but as a purification of the body, implying that the soul was already thoroughly cleansed by right behaviour." (Antiquities, XVIII, 117). Mark's 'baptism of repentance' suggests that the immersion itself effects repentance automatically and leads to the forgiveness of sins—the genitive is qualitative—'the repentance-immersion'. But Josephus here stresses John's insistence that right behaviour was necessary if repentance was to result in forgiveness, and that immersion only purifies the body cultically. This need of moral reform before baptism is supported by the report in Q (Matthew 3:7–10; Luke 3:7–9) of John's condemnation of some crowds who came for baptism. At Qumran there is a similar provision in Community Rule V that the men of falsehood "shall not enter the water or partake of the pure Meal of the saints, for they shall not be cleansed unless they turn from their wickedness:"—John is thought to have had links with the Qumran community.

This campaign of moral reform culminating in water baptism was undertaken by John to secure a verdict of 'not guilty' for people on the imminent Day of the Lord, God's Judgment Day. Purification by water has been a common practice in the history of religion, and cultic ablution (i.e. immersion in water to remove an impurity which would otherwise prevent entry to the Temple or contact with holy persons or things) is often enjoined in the Pentateuch. Thus, sexual discharges and intercourse necessitate bathing in water and waiting until evening, to remove the uncleanness (Leviticus 15). But this purification needs repeating after every occasion of uncleanness, and removes cultic, not moral, impurity. Moreover, John's baptism of repentance was available to Gentiles (e.g. the Roman soldiers at Luke 3:14), while the commandments at Sinai, including the rules of purity, were addressed only to the Israelites (and resident aliens).

Immersion in water was also an element in the ceremony marking the acceptance into Judaism of a Gentile (proselyte conversion); the other constituents were circumcision (for a man) , sacrifice, and the reading of provisions of the law. It has been doubted whether immersion had been incorporated into this ceremony early enough to influence John's baptismal practice. Yet for female converts immersion had presumably always been the essential part of the ceremony. It would be natural, however, for any Gentile to be required to immerse immediately after conversion in order to remove the impurity attaching to him or her by virtue of having been a Gentile, since all Gentiles were presumed to be impure. In addition to this logic, there is Rabbinic evidence that a bath was taken, and also that it was part of the ceremony of conversion. For, in the Mishnah (final composition c.200CE), the School of Shammai say that if a man became a proselyte on the day before Passover, he may immerse himself and consume his passover in the evening, but the School of Hillel say that as an ex-Gentile he suffers from corpse-impurity and must wait seven days (Pesah 8:8). This dispute indicates that immersion was necessary but was not part of the conversion ceremony. Most of the recorded disputes between the Houses stem from before CE70. A later dispute in the Babylonian Talmud indicates that immersion *was* part of the conversion ceremony:

Rabbi Joshua argued c.90CE that ritual ablution alone is sufficient to create a proper proselyte but the Sages say that both circumcision and ritual ablution are necessary (Yebamoth 46a).

Many think that this proselyte baptism was the precedent and model for John's baptism, but this seems to us unlikely. For it was a cultic cleansing due to Gentile impurity, and would have to be repeated whenever the proselyte became unclean again, whereas John's was a single immersion signifying moral reform. Further, although brought up in a priestly household, John's life was perhaps partly spent with the Qumran community but mainly in the desert, and the influence upon him of the practices of the synagogue would probably be less than that of the Scriptural prophets whose message of God's approaching vengeance was so similar to his own. Provisions such as Isaiah 1:16, "Wash yourselves; make yourselves clean; remove the evil of your doings from before my eyes;" and Ezekiel 36:25, "I will sprinkle clean water upon you, and you shall be clean from all your uncleannesses, and from all your idols I will cleanse you. A new heart I will give you, and a new spirit I will put within you;" are more likely to have been in John's mind when he conceived this new symbol of moral reform (cf. Zechariah 13:1; Psalm 51:7). Preference for this precedent is strengthened by the proselyte washing being, like all cultic immersions, with 'collected' water in a pool (mikveh) of not less than forty seahs, whereas John's immersions were in the flowing waters of the River Jordan.

Whatever be the exact precedent for John's baptism, it constituted 'a new thing' (cf. Isaiah 43:19) of great importance which provokes us to attempt to re-assess its author's position in Judaeo-Christian history.

The Gospels firmly subordinate him to Jesus of Nazareth, whom the Evangelists hail as the Messiah. Yet, notwithstanding this depreciation of John, the Evangelists devote a substantial part of their Gospels to material affecting him. After the title verse of his Gospel, Mark immediately speaks of John, while Luke who has a private source of John material, fills his first Chapter with the nativity story of John. The Evangelist John in his sixth verse acclaims the Baptist— "There was a man sent from God, whose name was John", and he starts his narrative with John's testimony. Matthew alone does not include information about John in his first Chapter. It is generally recognised that both the Evangelists and the early Christians from whom they obtained their information ('traditions'), adjusted their stories so as to increase their effectiveness as argument in their disputes with Judaism or within the Church. Thus, the Pharisees are painted as legalistic hypocrites, whereas the truth is that the majority, like Hillel and other Sages quoted in the Mishnaic 'Sayings of the Fathers' (Avoth), were sincere, selfless seekers of God's will. This antagonism probably arose because the Jews did not accept Jesus as the Messiah. Similarly, John's repeated subordination to Jesus in the Gospels probably arose from rivalry between his followers and those of Jesus. Unfortunately, we have no Gospels or other writings by John's disciples, but there is evidence of this rivalry in both the volume and the intensity of the depreciation of John in the Gospels. But notwithstanding this, some signs of John's eminence remain.

At Mark 1:7–8 after a description of John's ministry and lifestyle, John says, "After me comes he who is mightier than I, the thong of whose sandals I am not worthy to stoop down and untie." In view of John's later question from prison as to whether Jesus is the Messiah, it is probable that John is not referring to Jesus in this Marcan quotation. That John's disciples were a cohesive and rival group is indicated at 2:18, "Why do John's disciples fast... but your disciples do not fast?" and at Luke 11:1, "Lord, teach us to pray, as John taught his disciples." Perhaps the most fascinating assessment of John is that Herod and others thought that Jesus was the resurrected John (Mark 6:14–61), despite the difference in their lifestyles, John being ascetic and Jesus 'a glutton and a wine-bibber'. The explanation there that Jesus' powers (of healing and exorcism) derived from him being John redivivus is strong evidence that John, too, performed these works, though they are not mentioned in the Gospels. This idea that Jesus was a resurrected John is interestingly followed by the story of John's death through the wiles of Herodias, which ends with the report that his disciples "took his body and laid it in a tomb." (Mark 6:29). Is this intended to scotch any idea that John, like Jesus, was raised from the dead? John's prophetic moral zeal is shown by his condemnation of Herod's marriage reported here.

Luke at 3:1–14 includes his private material about John's ministry, and this too depicts his judgmental oratory and concern for moral reform. In similar vein to the Sermon on the Mount, John enjoins sharing of food and clothing, and urges honesty upon tax collectors and soldiers (interestingly, Gentiles). Significantly, Luke then adds that "all men questioned in their hearts concerning John, whether perhaps he were the Christ." The possibility seems to have been raised here for Luke to knock it down with John's 'thong of sandal' speech . The 'Q' source common to Matthew and Luke also has information about John at Luke 7:18–35 (par. Matthew 11:2–11). Any idea that John had recognised Jesus as the Messiah at an early stage is opposed, as mentioned above, by John's enquiry from prison at the start of this passage, as to whether Jesus is the Messiah ("he who is to come") or whether they should look for another. Clearly, the ordinary people were fascinated by John, for Jesus asks them what did they expect to see when they went to the wilderness after him. Again, Josephus gives as the reason for Herod's killing that Herod feared that John's eloquence would lead the crowds to sedition, such was the effect of his preaching (Antiquities XVIII, 118). Jesus then makes the statement so valued by John's supporters, "I tell you, among those born of women, none is greater than John;", yet Jesus snatches away the glory with the qualification, "yet he who is least in the kingdom of God is greater than he." (7:28). Taken literally, the first limb of this verse is the highest possible praise—no human ever born is greater than John! Contrary to John's view that he is unworthy to unloose Jesus' shoe, Jesus, being 'one born of a woman', here acknowledges that he is not greater than John; indeed may even be lesser. This elevation of John is hardly belittled by the second limb's rendering him inferior to the least in the kingdom, for those in the kingdom must be angels and other heavenly echelons since they are contrasted with "those born of women".

Some of John's disciples apparently relied on this saying of Jesus for their claim that John, and not Jesus, was the Christ. In the Recognitions of Clement, probably dating from early third century but containing much earlier material, it is stated , "And, behold, one of the disciples of John asserted that John was the Christ, and not Jesus, inasmuch as Jesus himself declared that John was greater than all men and all prophets. 'If then,' said that disciple, 'he be greater than all, he must be held to be greater than Moses and than Jesus himself. But if he be the greatest of all, then must he be the Christ." (LX cf. LIV).

There is evidence in the New Testament that John had, as mentioned above, his own group of disciples, and that the disciples continued to follow him after his death. At John 3:22–3 it is mentioned that Jesus remained with his disciples in Judea and baptized, and that John also was baptizing at Aenon near Salim, and at v.24 a dispute is reported between John's disciples and a Jew (probably Jesus) over purifying; interestingly, the Evangelist contradicts himself at 4:1 by saying that Jesus himself did not baptize, but only his disciples. At Acts 18 and 19 which relate events about 30 years after John's death, we read of disciples of John who had probably become his disciples after his death. Vv.24–8 of Ch.18 speak of Apollos, a Jew well versed in the scriptures, who knew only the baptism of John. At 19:1–7 Paul finds at Ephesus twelve disciples presumably of John since we are told they were baptized "unto John's baptism". In reply to Paul's query whether they had received the Holy Spirit, they say they had not even heard of it. Admittedly, two of John's disciples are reported at John 1:35–7 to desert John for Jesus, but the remainder presumably believed that John was a preferable spiritual leader to Jesus, and the remainder may have formed a large number; Josephus writes that the crowds "were aroused to the highest degree by his sermons... Eloquence that had so great an effect on mankind might lead to some form of sedition, for it looked as if they would be guided by John in everything that they did." (ibid.). In contrast, the Pharisees claimed that John had a demon (Luke 7:33).

Perhaps the highest assessment of John is contained in the Lucan infancy stories between 1:5 and 2:52. The elaborate dating of John's ministry at the start of Luke's Ch.3 (with which ministry Mark's Gospel starts) indicates that this was also the original beginning of Luke's Gospel and that Chs. 1 and 2 were added later. While the stories in Luke written around John's birth are probably legend surrounding a kernel of fact, they give many indications of having been copied by Luke from an Aramaic or Hebrew source. Echoes are present of the birth stories of Isaac, Samson and Samuel, a knowledge of Jewish customs affecting the priesthood is evident, and the grammatical constructions and sentence formations are often semitic. This source may well have originated with the disciples of John. Although this Lucan narrative mentions John as a prophet (1:76) and the new Elijah (1:17), John is also presented as the fore-runner of God and not of the Messiah. Verses 16 and 17 say that he will turn many of the sons of Israel to the Lord their God, and will go before him (i.e. God) in the spirit and power of Elijah. John is virtually cast as Messiah since he will "go before the Lord to prepare his ways" (v.76)—'Lord' in these verses translates the Greek word 'kurios' which is here the Greek translation of the Hebrew 'Yahweh', God the Father. John's birth is due to an act of divine intervention, he is filled with the Holy Spirit from his mother's womb (1:15), and through his birth God has already visited and redeemed his people and raised up a horn of salvation for them (vv.68–9). V.69 adds "in the house of his servant David", but this is a later Christian addition since Zechariah, a priest, is clearly speaking of his son, John; only Jesus was of the house of David. Clearly, the whole of this psalm, the Benedictus, refers to John.

Similarly, the Magnificat (vv.46–55) is attributed to Mary, but in the oldest Old Latin manuscripts the preface in v.46 is "And Elizabeth John's mother said"; at v.56 following we read "Mary stayed with her," but if Mary had uttered the Magnificat, we would expect, 'she stayed with Elizabeth'. Further, the Magnificat is based on the Song of Hannah at I Sam. 2:1–10, where Hannah praises God for her son, conceived like Elizabeth, after long barrenness. We see in these nativity narratives Christian arrogation to Jesus of material about John. Whatever be the historicity of the narratives, their very existence indicates that his followers placed John in an almost Messianic rôle.

"Who are you?" John was asked (John 1:19). We think the evidence in this study shows John to have been a revolutionary Jewish prophet in that he transformed an infinitely repeatable act of cultic cleansing into a once-for-all baptism signifying a repentance to lead to divine forgiveness. John's followers held him in such high esteem that the followers of Jesus strove in the Gospels to ensure that the supremacy of their leader was not endangered. Another example of their argumentation may be discerned at John 1:15; in the Synoptics John says that Jesus 'comes after me', so John's disciples may have claimed in accordance with Jewish thinking, that the earlier (John) has priority over the later (Jesus). John baptized Jesus and was thus the senior. Hence John the Evangelist there causes the Baptist to say, "He who comes after me ranks before me, for he was before me" (i.e. as pre-existent). It is disappointing that such rivalry was indulged at the very birth of Christendom, whose founder estimated the Baptizer so highly.

Nevertheless, John's influence on Christianity was formative. His use of a once-for-all immersion as the sign of repentance and moral reform was the matrix from which developed the baptismal practice of the Christian church. According to Acts 19:3-6 baptism in the name of John did not confer the Holy Spirit (God's beneficence), whereas baptism in the name of Jesus did. However, possession of the Holy Spirit is difficult to prove and this report may have been influenced by group rivalry.

The Hidden Years of Jesus

The Gospels tell us much about Jesus' birth and much about the last three years of his life which were the years of his ministry. But we know hardly anything about the almost twelve years between his being presented in the Temple and his visit to the Temple at age twelve with his parents. Nor do we know anything about the eighteen years between that visit to the Temple and his being baptized by John the Baptist, which was followed by his temptations in the wilderness and the commencement of his ministry.

Only Luke tells us about the presentation of Jesus as a baby in the Temple and the visit to the Temple twelve years later with his parents. Luke was a Gentile born in Antioch and it is interesting that although a Gentile he stresses in these incidents how Jesus was brought up in conformity with the provisions of the Jewish laws. Luke wrote his Gospel in about 85 CE.

He mentions how Jesus was circumcised on the 8th day and how at the same time the name Jesus was given to him. Circumcision was commanded at Leviticus (12:2) following God's command to Abraham. This was done at home. Also Exodus 13 required that the first-born males should be consecrated to the Lord, in memory of God's sparing of the Israelite first-born at the slaughter of the first-born in Egypt when Pharaoh refused to let the Israelites leave Egypt. The intention was that the first-born should spend his life serving the Lord as Samuel did in the Temple. But the Levites eventually took over this serving of the Lord in the Temple. So in Numbers (8:15–16) it was provided that the first-born could be bought back from the service of the Lord for 5 shekels payable at the Temple. But there was no obligation to bring the child to the Temple for this presentation and payment. The third stipulation of the Jewish law after a birth was the purification of the mother. Luke refers to 'their' purification but it only affected the mother. Leviticus (12) provides that the mother of a male child shall be unclean for forty days which meant that she was disqualified from any form of public worship. At the end of this time she had to make the prescribed sacrifices in the Temple. Luke reports that Jesus' parents observed all these legal provisions and he thereby indicates that Jesus was brought up in a law-observant family.

After these observances and the meeting with the aged Simeon and Hannah at Jesus' presentation in the Temple, nothing is reported about Jesus until Luke's report of the family visit to Jerusalem for the Passover festival when Jesus was 12. The information which Luke gives about the first visit to the Temple and this second visit for the Passover comes from Luke's private source of information. However, Mark, Matthew and John do not mention it. There is no shortage of fanciful tales in Gospels not contained in the New Testament. In the Infancy Gospel of Thomas, it is stated that Jesus made clay sparrows on the Sabbath, and when upbraided by Joseph for doing this, Jesus told the sparrows to fly away which they did. Again, when Jesus was eight, Joseph was ordered by a customer to construct a bed for him and when Joseph having cut two pieces of wood, found that one was too short, Jesus took the short piece and stretched it to the length of the other. But such are the stories gathered about the childhood of famous people in ancient times.

Jesus parents went every year to the Passover in Jerusalem, another sign of their conformity with Jewish custom. The law required attendance at the Temple for the three festivals of Passover, Weeks and Tabernacles. But most Galileans went only to Passover, due to the distance between Jerusalem and Galilee. It is possible that Jesus was celebrating his 'bar mitzvah' on this visit. A Jewish boy became a 'bar mitzvah', a son of the law, at the first signs of manhood, although later the age was fixed at 13. From his bar mitzvah, a boy was obliged to fulfil the provisions of the law and to commemorate this, a service was held in the synagogue at which the boy read the day's passage from the law. But Jesus would have been familiarised with the law from earliest childhood by being taught to read the Hebrew text in the synagogue school.

It is, therefore, not so surprising that Jesus should be found in the Temple listening to the scribes' discussion and asking questions. What is surprising is his answer to his mother's complaint, 'my son, why have you treated us like this? Your father and I have been searching for you in great anxiety.' For Jesus replied, 'What made you search? Did you not know that I was bound to be in my Father's house?' It is interesting that we have here references to both Jesus' human father Joseph, and his heavenly Father.

After this second visit to the Temple at age 12, we have a news blackout in the Gospels until Jesus is baptized by John in the Jordan, followed by his temptations in the wilderness. Luke tells us that Jesus was 30 when he began his ministry which probably means at his baptism. So there are 18 years of which we have no direct knowledge.

In Mark (6:3), "the people wonder where Jesus has obtained his healing powers from and they ask, 'Is not this the carpenter, the son of Mary?'" Some manuscripts have "is not this the son of the carpenter and Mary", but the majority manuscripts have "the carpenter the son of Mary" and there is strong tradition that Jesus was a carpenter. The Greek word used in the Gospels is '*tekton*' meaning a carpenter or worker in wood. It is probable that Joseph was a carpenter as Matthew indicates that Jesus learned his trade from his father (13:55).

If Luke's source of information is correct, we deduce from it that Jesus was brought up in a typically observant Jewish home as his parents observed the requirements affecting childbirth and attendance at Passover. We can also deduce from his staying behind to listen to and question the scribes that Jesus had developed at an early age a considerable knowledge of the Jewish law, the Torah. The Torah comprised the Hebrew Scriptures, largely the Old Testament, and the decisions of the scribes interpreting those laws for subsequent generations.

This youthful background of Jesus is helpful in understanding the attitude towards the Jewish law shown in his later ministry and teaching. Paul wrote that Christ was the end of the law and people have portrayed Jesus as opposed to the law. But Jesus as a well-brought up Jew observed the law, and his arguments with the scribes were over its interpretation particularly over the interpretation of the Sabbath laws. He, too, honoured the Sabbath commandment but denied that healing came within the definition of 'work' on the Sabbath. He did not deny that certain foods going into a man defiled him. He claimed that things going into a man didn't defile <u>as much as</u> things going out such as greed, malice, arrogance and slander.

Five

There is some evidence that Jesus originally chose five disciples to form a group closer to him than his other followers. In Sanhedrin (43a), the Talmud records a 'baraitha' (a saying of a Rabbi before 200 CE) that "Yeshu (Jesus) had five disciples, Matthai, Nakai, Nezer, Buni and Todah." (This baraitha immediately follows another baraitha about the 'hanging' of Jesus.)

Matthai is thought to be an Aramaic form of Matthew, Nakai of Luke; Nezer means a Nazorean; Buni means John; and Todah, Thaddaeus. Matthew, John and Thaddaeus are included in Mark's list of twelve (3:16–19).

Support for an original five comes from the Gospels of Mark and John. The disciples whose recruiting ("Follow me") is reported in Mark's first two Chapters number five, Simon and Andrew, James and John, and Levi. In John's Gospel, Jesus also recruits five disciples. In Chapter 1, two disciples (of whom one is Andrew) standing with John the Baptist, follow Jesus. Andrew then brings his brother, Peter, to Jesus. The next day Jesus recruits Philip and Nathaniel.

The brothers, Simon Peter and Andrew, are the only two names in both the Gospel quintets, and only John appears in a Talmudic and a Gospel quintet (Mark's). It is pertinent that in both Mark and John, after Jesus' enlistment of the five, the narrative passes to other matters and there are no further callings until the appointment of the Twelve to "be with him".

The identity of the five is confusing in these accounts, particularly since in the Talmud one is only called a Nazorean, and in John one is only defined as a fellow disciple with Andrew, of John the Baptist. The significant feature in each account is the number five. Perhaps an original smaller group of five close disciples expanded into twelve through Jesus' discovery of new candidates as his ministry progressed and his followers increased.

Certainly, the Gospel evidence that at some stage in the ministry there was a group of twelve disciples, seems strong. The fact that Matthew, Mark and Luke each report the choosing of twelve, yet state slightly different members, indicates that they may each have gleaned their report of an appointment of twelve, from different sources.

The Transfiguration (Mark 9)

Moses told the Israelites that God would raise up for them a prophet like him and that they should heed him. And God said "I will put my words in his mouth." (Deuteronomy, 13:15).

Christians believe that God here was speaking of Jesus, and it is most appropriate that Moses appears in the Transfiguration story both for this reason and as representing the law given on Mount Sinai. And God gave here the test for discerning the true prophet—does His word come true?

Some say the appearance of Jesus on the mountain at the Transfiguration was a retrojection, a putting back a post-resurrection appearance into the human life of Jesus. Mark's account of the Transfiguration is followed fairly closely by Matthew and Luke. So we probably have only one independent witness for the story because Luke and Matthew have largely copied Mark.

There are, however realistic details which support the authenticity of the story. Peter did not know what to say, understandably so, they were terrified, says Mark. He offers to build three tents for them. Perhaps there is a play on words here with the Greek for 'tents' and 'Shekinah' for the presence of God. The story may have been received by Mark from Peter.

The metamorphosis of Jesus and the appearances of Moses and Elijah were probably visionary being very similar; Matthew thought so for he called it a vision in his account (Greek, horama).

Some think that only Peter experienced the vision since shared visions are rare. It is interesting that this vision occurred soon after Peter's acknowledgement of Jesus as Messiah in the previous Marcan chapter. In the Bible God often communicates with people in dreams and visions. In the Old Testament Ezekiel, Jeremiah and Amos are examples and in the New Testament, the visions of Mary and Joseph and of John of Patmos who wrote the Book of Revelation are examples. This has strong claim to be a God-inspired vision for not only are Jesus' clothes glistening white, just as the clothes of the young man at the empty tomb were shining white. Similarly, the Shekinah, the divine presence, is indicated by the cloud as in Exodus, "Behold the glory of the Lord appeared in the cloud," (16:10).

God's authorisation of Jesus as his spokesman is shown in the words from the cloud, "This is my son, my Beloved, listen to him." They confirm the words to Jesus at his baptism, "Thou art my Son, my Beloved."

These words sanction Jesus' teachings as coming from God. Moses represents the law given to him on another mountain, Sinai, and Elijah represents the prophets. When the bath qol says "listen to him" it vindicates Jesus' teaching as a culmination and completion of the law and the prophets. The vision then ceased, and Jesus was alone with the three disciples. A bath qol was very occasionally claimed to have been heard by the Rabbis and to have pronounced who was correct in their discussions, but these, too, may have been auditory visions.

Strangely, Jesus on the way down the mountain instructs the disciples not to tell anyone until the Son of man had risen from the dead. Is this a clue to suggest that the vision did appear after the Resurrection? The question "Why do the scribes say that first Elijah must come?" (Mark 9: 10) may have been asked on another occasion but is put here by Mark because of the connection with Elijah. It relates to Malachi 4: 5, "Behold I will send you Elijah the prophet before the great and terrible day of the Lord comes." So the thinking behind the disciples' question is, "If the kingdom is about to arrive, should not Elijah have come to earth by now since the scribes say he must come to herald the kingdom?" Jesus replies that Elijah has already come and they worked their will upon him. Mark adds that the disciples understood that by Elijah, Jesus meant John the Baptist. Mark inserts into the middle of Jesus' reply here, "Yet how is it that the scriptures say of the Son of man that he is to endure great sufferings and to be treated with contempt?" a further piece of evidence suggesting that Jesus did think of himself as the Suffering Servant described in Isaiah (53).

Pentecost: "What Does This Mean?" (Acts 2:12)

Many, upon hearing the Whit Sunday story, may be 'amazed and perplexed' at the babble of languages, and wonder with those Jews at the Pentecost festival, shortly after the Ascension, "What does this mean?" (v.12).

To answer the question we must try to discover to what extent Luke (the author of Acts) was simply reporting what, according to his informants, actually happened, and to what extent he or they were influenced by a desire to recognise in the event the fulfilment of Hebrew scripture and to establish a foundation date for the Christian Church.

There are several distinct elements in the story as Luke tells it:

1. The disciples were present in Jerusalem at the Feast of Weeks which was celebrated seven weeks (or 50 days, hence Pentecost, meaning in Greek, fifty) after the Feast of Passover and Unleavened Bread. It marked the conclusion of the wheat harvest, and was a joyful time, which might partly explain the allegation of drunkenness (Acts 2:13). Two loaves of bread were presented in the Temple as an offering of first-fruits .The Jewish feasts thus began as agricultural festivals but were later historicised. The Feast of Weeks came to celebrate the covenants between God and Noah, and God and Abraham and, after the destruction of the Temple in 70 CE, the giving of the law at Sinai. Luke's story does not seem to draw on this background.

2. The phenomena of wind and tongues of fire suggest the presence of God. The Hebrew 'ruach' and the Greek 'anemos' used for 'the spirit of God' mean both 'wind' and 'spirit'(cf. John 3:8). In early times, Yahweh was known as a God of thunder, storm and wind, and the angel of the Lord appeared to Moses in a flame of fire in the bush (Exodus 3:2).

3. But the tongues of fire also suggest the Last Judgment. John the Baptist declared, "He who is coming after me will baptise you with the Holy Spirit and with fire" (Matthew 3:11).

4. The speaking with tongues is the most prominent element, and Peter in Acts (2:17) demonstrates from the

prophet Joel how this was prophesied to happen in the Last Days (Joel 2:28–32).

Clearly something momentous and significant must have happened at that Pentecost to have initiated Luke's story, and vv.4 to 18 constitute good evidence that it was the speaking in different national languages which provoked it. But what did speaking in other tongues entail? Luke understands it here to mean speaking in foreign languages so that the assembled Jews from Asian and Mediterranean countries all recognised their own language. Although they came from a wide area, most of them would understand Aramaic or Koine Greek, but Luke clearly means native languages. Perhaps Luke had the reversal of Babel in mind–that God having caused the peoples to separate because they could not understand each other at Babel (Genesis 11:1–9), would unite them through the universal mission of the Church.

However, it is likely that the language was the 'glossolalia', that ecstatic utterance, often unintelligible, which has been a feature of charismatic Christianity from Paul's day (1 Corinthians 14) to the present.

We suggest that one of the disciples present, or a passer-on (tradent) of the story, or more likely Luke himself (since the Greek Bible is quoted), has noticed the connection between this speaking in tongues and the words of Joel at (2:28), "And it shall come to pass afterward that I will pour out my spirit on all flesh; your sons and your daughters shall prophesy."

Luke, when putting these words in the mouth of Peter, substitutes "in the last days" for Joel's "afterward" since Joel has been speaking in the previous verses about the restoration of Israel in the Last Days after the plague of locusts. Joel's Hebrew verb in verse 28 translated as "prophesy" ('naba') and the Greek verb (propheteuo) in Luke's Greek Bible do not mean in this context predicting the future but utterance in religious ecstasy which is comparable to the dreams of the old men and the visions of the young men later in Joel's verse and all is the result of the pouring of the spirit in the Last Days, "I will give portents in the heavens and on the earth, blood and fire and columns of smoke. The sun shall be turned to darkness, and the moon to blood before the great and terrible day of the Lord comes." (Joel 2: 30–31)

His imagination having been kindled by the 'tongues', Luke may have imported into the occasion from Joel the pouring of the spirit, the fire and the eschatology.

Whether God's force (the Holy Spirit) did enter the disciples is a subjective issue upon which only they could speak, but the speaking in tongues is certainly attested elsewhere as a consequence of the entry of the spirit. When Moses found the burden of leading the Israelites through the wilderness too heavy for him alone, God took some of the spirit that was on Moses and put it upon the seventy elders, and they 'prophesied' (Numbers 11:25). The Hebrew verb translated 'prophesied' is the same 'naba' (although a different conjugation) and has the same nuance of ecstatic utterance. Again, after Saul's anointing as king by Samuel, a band of prophets met him "and the spirit of God came mightily upon him, and he prophesied (Hebrew, naba) among them." (1 Samuel 10:10).

Luke's evidence that the Jewish disciples spoke in foreign languages is opposed by the unlikelihood of their knowledge of this wide range of languages. But if we interpret the 'other tongues' as glossolalia, this objection to Luke's evidence is removed. We have recorded a sample of the evidence that in the view of the biblical writers the impact of the spirit of God caused glossolalia. That the disciples thus spoke in tongues seems proved, but that the spirit of God caused it, while alleged by the biblical writers, is unprovable.

The sequence of Luke's composition of the Pentecost story may have been that he received a tradition simply of the speaking in foreign languages at Pentecost, but was reminded thereby of the passage in Joel linking the outpouring of the spirit in the Last Days and the attendant fire, to ecstatic utterance. He then skilfully wove these elements into the initial tradition, adding the reference to the wind as verbally linked in Hebrew and Greek with spirit.

Since Jesus' promise of the Holy Spirit is only made in Luke's work (24:49 and Acts 1:5 ; in John's Gospel Jesus confers the Spirit before the Ascension (20:22)), it seems on a balance of probability that Luke, interpreting the glossolalia as the work of the Spirit occurring shortly after the Ascension, believed that Jesus would have mentioned it earlier, so included the promise of it in those two verses. Certainly, according to Luke, the outpouring of the Spirit at Pentecost on the disciples was followed by a communal life which demonstrated the marks of the Spirit (Acts 2:42–47). It is not, therefore, surprising that the Pentecost event, coming shortly after the Ascension, has been identified by Christians as the birthday of the Church.

Do Not Worry!

We possess different temperaments, some people are carefree by nature—with a sunny disposition little seems to bother them.

Others can always find something to worry about, it's as if there's a little box in their brain marked 'worry', and it has to be kept filled up with some worry all the time—as one worry is disposed of, another has to take its place.

"You cannot serve God and Money," says Jesus (Matthew 6:24), and no doubt many worries arise from the needless pursuit of Money or Mammon. But Jesus goes much further than that. He bids us put away anxious thoughts about food and drink to keep us alive, and clothes to cover our body. His Father will look after us, and as proof of this he cites the case of the birds – they don't sow or reap and yet his Father feeds them.

Similarly with the lilies, they don't work, yet their clothes are more splendid than Solomon's. This is probably a genuine teaching of Jesus because it is taken by both Matthew and Luke from the sayings source 'Q', a collection of sayings of Jesus written in 50 CE, about 15 years before Mark's Gospel was written. We have good reason to believe that these sayings about anxiety come from Q because they are not in Mark's Gospel and yet both Matthew and Luke contain the sayings in nearly identical Greek wording.

However, these sayings about not worrying about our lives, food, drinks and clothes are difficult because our heavenly Father doesn't feed all the birds and animals of his creation—many of them die of starvation. This is perhaps the ruling principle behind Darwin's theory of Natural Selection in that nature governs the development of the species since only those who are the strongest live long enough to pass on their genes. It is also true of humankind for millions in Africa and the East die of starvation. They, indeed, have reason to be anxious.

Jesus continues, "Set your mind on God's Kingdom and His justice before everything else, and all the rest will come to you as well. So do not be anxious about tomorrow; tomorrow will look after itself. Each day has troubles enough of its own." Here again a difficult teaching. Should we not save for the rainy day?

Should we not pay into pension schemes so that when we retire we can live without being a burden to our family or fellow citizens? Yet Jesus repeats the example of the birds, they don't store away in barns for the future in the way that we store away in investments and pension schemes. (The squirrel is an exception!)

Jesus' instruction to us to not to bother about tomorrow seems foolhardy, surely we ought to make reasonable plans for the future. Jesus, himself, in other places commends prudence and practical wisdom. In Luke 14 we read, "Which of you desiring to build a tower, does nor first sit down and count the cost whether he has enough to complete it? Otherwise when he has laid a foundation, and is not able to finish, all who see it begin to mock him saying, 'this man began to build and was not able to finish? Or what king going to encounter another king in war, will not first sit down and take counsel whether he is able with ten thousand to meet him who comes against him with twenty thousand? And if not, while the other is yet a great way off, he sends an embassy and asks terms of peace." And in Saying 89 of the Gospel of Thomas Jesus links the Kingdom to a man wanting to kill a powerful man. He first checks his sword to see if his hand can carry it through, and then slays him.

So perhaps Jesus in urging us not to worry about the morrow, is exaggerating. After all, he did say that if we had faith equal to a grain of mustard seed, we could move a mountain, and that it's easier for a camel to go through the eye of a needle than for a rich man to enter the kingdom of heaven. Perhaps he is telling us in a dramatic way that it's all right to have prudent plans for the future but having made plans, we should dismiss the subject from our minds less it begins to preoccupy us and drive from our minds the things that should be concerning us.

105

He then gives us the secret to prevent our minds being besieged by worldly worries after we have made reasonable plans—set your minds on God's kingdom and His justice before everything else and all the rest will come to you as well. If we then give our minds to furthering God's kingdom which means helping and cheering others, our minds will be so full of worthwhile thoughts and aspirations that there will be no room for excessive worry and anxiety about self. Excessive anxiety benumbs the mind, and as Jesus asks, can one of us by anxious thought add a foot to his stature? (Matthew 6:27).

Prayer and trust in God are the best antidote to worry, as Paul wrote in his letter to the Christians at Philippi:-

"The Lord is near. Do not worry about anything. but in everything by prayer and supplication with thanksgiving, let your requests be made known to God."

The result may be seen in the lines of a popular song which bears our adaptation of it—

> *"Happy days are here again, God's will has been revealed to men.*
> *If we love him and our neighbour too, then his kingdom will flow through.*
> *When we find someone in need and bring a glow when he feels low,*
> *We have sown a seed, as the Son decreed, and the Father makes it grow.*
> *If helping others we try, our selfish worries will fly.*
> *Though we'll have our share of care. Yet Jesus will be always there.*
> *So we thank the Lord for this reward—Happy days are here again!"*

'Doing and Believing'

Christians are split up into separate groups (denominations) by different shades of belief about such matters as the composition of the Godhead and the redemptive effect of the death of Jesus (e.g. "the lamb of God that taketh away the sins of the world.").

Jesus was brought up as a traditional Jew, and inherited much of the Jewish religious approach. The essential belief of Israel was that there was one true God (Deuteronomy 6:4); the remainder of religion consisted in loving God and our neighbour. This love was shown by doing His will as it was revealed in the laws given to Moses. The relevance of some of these laws, such as the dietary, to the spiritual life may be elusive to Gentiles, but the observant Jew delights to keep all the commandments as an opportunity of showing his love for God,

"Oh, how I love thy law! It is my meditation all the day." wrote the Psalmist (119:97).

Jesus gave a similar preference to people doing the will of his Father rather than honouring himself. "Why do you call me Lord," he asked, "and not do what I tell you?" (Luke 6:46). And to the woman who proclaimed the blessedness of the womb that bore him, he replied, "Blessed, rather, are those who hear the word of God and keep it." (Luke 11:27–28).

The change from Jewish emphasis on God-serving behaviour to Gentile preoccupation with qualifying beliefs about the person (status) of Jesus arose after his death. Jesus had preached the good news of his Father's Kingdom and that people could enter it if they allowed God's will to reign in their hearts. The early Christians after his death, instead of repeating that good news, preached about the person of Jesus and his resurrection.

With the spread of Christianity into the Gentile world Greek-oriented thinkers concentrated on the formulation of dogmas about Jesus' pre-existence and the co-existence of the divine and the human in the same person

This approach was far removed from the practical religion of Jesus, and conflict, even persecution, over issues of 'correct' belief have stained the annals of Christian history. The lesson of this history is surely that we should welcome as fellow-Christians all who try to base their 'doing' on Jesus' teaching. Let the Christian bond be not a uniformity of belief, but a common aspiration to follow that teaching.

Pioneers and Martyrs

The Christians who have interpreted Scripture differently from the hitherto accepted 'orthodoxy', have in many cases not only exercised fine intellect in their pursuit of truth, but also great courage. For they suffered much for their persistence in proclaiming their views in the-face of a hostile ecclesiastical establishment. They were in this sense martyrs as well as pioneers. There is rueful irony in the feature that all were accused of heresy in their day, yet now their views are accepted among the standard interpretations of Scripture.

(1) J. M. Campbell

A worthy example is J.M. Campbell. Born in 1800, he studied for the ministry at Glasgow University, and was then inducted to the parish of Rhu on the Gare Loch.

Although a faithful pastor there for 5 years or so, some parishioners objected to passages in his sermons on the ground that they contravened the Confession of Faith then prevailing in the Church of Scotland. This confession embodied the Calvinist doctrine that Christ died for the elect only. Thus, at Mark (13:20), Jesus is reported to say that no human being would be saved in the last days if the Lord had not shortened the days for the sake of the elect, and that in those days the Son would gather His elect from the ends of the earth (27). But notes taken by his parishioners showed that Campbell had said, "God loves every child of Adam with a love the measure of which is the agony of his own Son." and, "The person who knows that Christ died for every human being is the person who is in a condition to go forth to every human being and say, "Let there be peace between you and God!"

This universalist teaching proclaimed that God through his Son's crucifixion enabled all men to be reconciled to Him for he bore the sins of the world. In an all-night sitting, the General Assembly of the Church adjudicated on the charges and by 119 to 6, Campbell was held to have taught doctrines at variance with the Word of God and the standards of the Church of Scotland. He was deposed from the sacred ministry.

Unbroken by this severe sentence, Campbell worked for many years as pastor of an independent congregation in

Glasgow. During this time he preached that it was not just the restriction of the benefit of Christ's saving death to the elect, that was mistaken, but rather the whole judicial basis of an atonement whereby God as judge required his Son to accept the punishment for the sins of mankind, as their substitute. This was a legal fiction, an intellectual construct. So he abandoned the idea of Christ dying as a penal substitute for men generally, and taught that God should be seen as a loving Father rather than a judge; instead, men would be justified by participation in the life of Christ, like the branches of the vine.

By being thus 'in Christ' (cf. Paul) Christians could share in the sufferings of Christ, and if they themselves were suffering, the idea of Christ suffering as their substitute, falls to the ground. Campbell published these views and many more in 1865 in a book, 'The Nature of the Atonement' which has been described as "the most systematic and masterly book on the work of Christ produced by a British theologian in the 19th century. This book was a factor leading to the modification of the form of Assent to the Confession of Faith. Sadly, this justification of the saintly 'heretic' was not enacted until after his death in 1872.

(2) John William Colenso

In the parish church of St. Austell in Cornwall, there is a stained glass window dedicated to J.W. Colenso by "his fellow townsmen and friends" four years after his death in 1883. The text engraved on the window is Matthew (26:65), "Then the High Priest rent his clothes, saying, "He hath spoken blasphemy. What further need have we of witnesses? Behold ye have heard his blasphemy", and the window depicts this scene.

The text is ironically appropriate since Colenso, too, was considered by the ecclesiastical establishment of his day to have committed heresy; he was deposed from his bishopric, and excommunicated. How did all this come about?

Born in 1814 at St. Austell, his father was part owner of a tin mine which was flooded by the sea, and the family lost their main income. His mother died when he was 16, and John worked as a school usher at Dartmouth to raise the money for his brothers' schooling. His uncle and grandmother enabled him to attend Cambridge University, and his brilliance at mathematics (second Wrangler) secured him a college fellowship. He then left to teach mathematics at Harrow, where through his boarding house he was saddled with even more debt, which he ultimately discharged through his authorship of successful maths textbooks for schools. Having been ordained at age 25, he became Rector of Forncett in Norfolk through the influence of his wife's family.

Forncett was in the rural Deanery of Depwade, and there is early evidence of Colenso's thinking in the minutes of the Depwade Clerical Society. In a paper on 1 Timothy 2:3–4 in 1846 he asserted universalism, "We have all received life from Him. This love of God towards His entire Intelligent Creation is confirmed by Analogy of Nature: the rain from Heaven and fruitful seasons."

Colenso had been much influenced by the liberal views of his friend, F.D. Maurice, and in defence of his friend he argued that modern science led one to a far deeper understanding of God and His creation. He also argued that it was wrong to uproot altogether the old religion of the heathen mind; prophetic words from the future missionary.

Colenso had wanted to be a missionary for some years, and as he had paid off his debts through sale of his copyrights, he felt able to accept the offer from Bishop Gray (Cape Town) of the new bishopric of Natal and was consecrated in 1853. The Zulu language then formed a barrier to evangelism, but in less than three months after his arrival Colenso was advertising his English Dictionary, Zulu Grammar and revised version in Zulu of Matthew's Gospel! In his first seven years there he had also translated the entire New Testament and Genesis, Exodus and Samuel in the Old and published other works in Zulu. In addition to this he had established a model mission-station with press, school, theological college, farm smithy, church, etc!

It was during the translation of Genesis and Exodus that William Ngidi, one of his African assistants, raised doubts in the Bishop's mind concerning the historical veracity and, therefore, divine inspiration of everything in the Old Testament. Ngidi enquired whether Colenso really believed that Noah could have fitted all the creatures into the ark described in Genesis. Moreover, Colenso perceived that geological discoveries showed it to be very unlikely that the flood had covered the whole world. His zest for arithmetical accuracy in his 18 Biblical calculations compounded his scepticism. For example, he showed that, giving each person space of 18 x 24 inches and placing the size of the outer tabernacle of the Temple at 1692 square yards and the number of male Israelites at 603,550 (Numbers 1:45), there was not room to accommodate the whole congregation alleged at Leviticus 8:4 to have been assembled there. He even pointed to the inaccuracy of the cud-chewing hare in Leviticus (11:6)! Colenso believed that his disproof of the verbal inspiration of the Bible would help evangelism by showing that the Bible should not be treated as unchallengeable history, but as "containing a message from God to our souls". These views were set out in Part 1 of his 'Pentateuch and Joshua' published in 1862, but he had already horrified the Anglican establishment by his publication in 1861 of St. Paul's Epistle to the Romans, newly translated and explained from a missionary point of view. Here he explained the Gospel, which he thought, should be preached to the 'heathens'. He interpreted Romans Chapter 1 as showing that God loves and has revealed himself to all humanity, and that to offer 'the heathen' a choice between conversion and damnation was an attempt to frighten them into faith. Further, the true view of Atonement was not that Christ died to appease a fierce Father demanding his pound of flesh but to "pay the debt of nature which sin had a right to demand of Him"; his death redeems everyone whether they have heard of Christ or not. He stressed the incarnation and the manhood of Jesus rather than the atonement, and was accused of Unitarian tendencies.

In 1863, Bishop Robert Gray, the Metropolitan of Cape Town, claimed to exercise jurisdiction over Colenso, whom he had appointed, and commenced proceedings in his church court to depose C (Colenso) from his bishopric on the strength of heresies alleged in C's writings. C protested against Gray's right to try him, but Gray pronounced deposition, and when C. ignored this, he excommunicated C – 'to be taken of the whole multitude of the faithful as a heathen man and a publican.' C then appealed to the Crown, and in March 1866, the Judicial Committee of the Privy Council gave judgment for C on the technical ground, that at the time Gray did not possess power to depose or excommunicate C. So, no judgment was given on his alleged heresies.

Notwithstanding the Privy Council's quashing of Gray's actions, various church and missionary authorities, resenting the Crown's right to over-rule a church court, treated C as deposed and excommunicated. After C's deposition, the trustees of the Colonial Bishoprics Fund suspended payment of C's stipend, and even after the Privy Council's reversal of the deposition, refused to restore the stipend, causing C to sue Gladstone (treasurer) and the trustees successfully. Several of the clergy vehemently opposed C, and on his return to Natal after the Privy Council case, the cathedral doors were locked against him. C was obliged to bring successive Court actions to restrain the Dean from barring his access to the cathedral. Gray and the Dean were supported by Canterbury and most English bishops, SPG and SPCK. Finally, schism occurred when, following C's success in the Chancery Court recognising the validity of his position and his entitlement to stipend, Gray took steps for the appointment of another Bishop who was to be in Pietermaritzburg but was to be a bishop of the new Church of South Africa, constituted by Gray, and not of the Church of England in South Africa. So there were two bishops, two cathedrals and two opposing congregations in the same city! Both factions claimed the ownership of the church assets, but after more litigation C was confirmed in possession of these. He had always been known in Natal by the Africans as 'Sobantu', the 'father of the people', and his concern for their welfare was to alienate in his later years those white settlers who had previously been his supporters. In 1873, some tribesmen brought home some guns they had been given, instead of money, for working in the diamond fields. Langalibalele, their tribal chief, afraid of treachery, refused to appear to answer the summons to Pietermaritzburg. The tribe were then hunted out of their location by the colonial authority, many killed, and the chief was tried and his death sentence commuted to transportation for life. C protested, and facts then discovered showed that the chief had good cause for his fear of treachery. C came to England, brought the whole matter before the Foreign Secretary, and obtained redress for the chief. He also sought justice for the Zulu king, Cetshwayo, when the false alarm of

112

a Zulu invasion was raised and the British High Commissioner urged the case for attack. C argued strenuously against this, but at Isandhlwana the British were heavily defeated. Despite his deep unpopularity with the authorities, C spoke severely in a famous sermon (1879) about the British treatment of the Zulus and the annexation of the Transvaal. He continued to fight for the restoration of the usurped Cetshwayo, despite his health declining through work and anxiety. He died in 1883.

Admittedly, C could be difficult and obstinate, but that a man who propagated views on the historicity of the Old Testament and the interpretation of the New, which are today accepted by so many, should have been excommunicated by the Church, condemned by his fellow bishops and ostracised by former friends, illustrates the suffering which often afflicts the pioneer.

Following his early mentor, F D Maurice, C was passionate about the need for unity not only in the Anglican Church, but between all churches, and, like Richard Baxter, longed for a comprehensive national church. This flowed, perhaps, from his universalism—that God is the loving Father of all.

Postscript. In 2003, the Church of South Africa endeavoured to make amends for C's treatment by a ceremonial revocation of his excommunication.

(3) Socrates, the great Athenian philosopher, lived from 470 to 399B.C., more than 400 years before Jesus, yet despite this difference there are interesting similarities in their careers, considered from a human point of view.

Neither of them wrote anything themselves, so we have to rely on third parties for the accuracy of what they taught. Plato preserved Socrates' teaching by writing dialogues in which one of the fictional characters questioned the other in the same way that Socrates would start a discussion by asking someone he met in the market-place a question such as 'what is virtue?' or 'what is courage?' Similarly, Jesus' teaching was only preserved because stories about his teaching and healing were passed on by the witnesses and then written down by the Evangelists. So in the case of both of them we cannot be sure that we have their exact words, or perhaps even their exact thoughts. (see pp. 9-10)

They both tried to make people think for themselves. Socrates, having received an answer to his question would then, by asking further questions, demonstrate that the original answer to his question could not be correct. This naturally irritated people, and he became known as 'the Gadfly' who was liable to sting through his questioning. Jesus, too, tried to make people think for themselves. He persisted with 'But you, who do *you* say that I am?' (Mark 8:29)

Their motivation was rather similar. Jesus had a close relationship with his heavenly Father whom he believed had commissioned him to declare the good news that the Kingdom of God was at hand. To a less intense extent Socrates believed that he had to continue his clarifying of the minds of his followers because a divine voice urged him on.

Both were put on trial for their teaching – Socrates for impiety towards the Greek Gods and for corrupting the minds of the young. One of the charges against Jesus, according to Luke, was perverting the nation (Luke 13:2). Socrates was as innocent as Jesus of the charges against him. It is interesting that while Jesus declined to answer before Pilate. Socrates did make a speech in his own defence, but when found guilty did not ask for the penalty of death to be alleviated, nor did he leave the country as he could have done. He drank hemlock in obedience to the Court's order.

Although there is no evidence that Socrates appeared like Jesus in a spiritual form after his death, he did believe in the immortality of the soul and dramatically declared how at his death his soul would leave his body.

Thus the comparisons on a human level between Jesus and Socrates are interesting, yet for Christians Jesus has a unique rôle in the revelation of God to man. However, we can justly honour those selfless

114

beings who have sought to improve the lot of their fellows and have submitted to martyrdom in that cause.

Chapter 7
Unitarian Christianity—A Singular Pedigree

Christianity sprang from Judaism because Jesus was a Jew. The Jews have always believed very firmly that God is One Person, and in their daily prayers they recite the Shema (the Hebrew for 'hear'), the first word of Deuteronomy (6:4), "Hear, O Israel: the Lord our God, the Lord, is one." Some concession to this primary principle was suspected when, in post-Biblical times, the Memra (the Word of God) and the Metatron (the interpreting angel) were recognised as agents of God, communicating God's will to man. But it was argued that these did not infringe God's unity because, like personified Wisdom in the Old Testament, they were created by God and were, therefore, inferior to him.

In the Synoptic Gospels (Matthew, Mark and Luke), Jesus speaks and refers to God as another person, his Father. This he does in a very natural way. The Lord's Prayer is an obvious example. It is true that in John's Gospel, Jesus says, "I and the Father are one." (10:30), and "before Abraham was, I am." (8:58). But the content and atmosphere of John's Gospel are so different from the Synoptics, that many of Jesus' sayings in it are now considered to be the expression of John's own meditations about the status of Jesus, rather than Jesus' own historical words. Admittedly, at Matthew (11:27), Jesus asserts: "All things have been delivered to me by my Father; and no one knows the Son except the Father, and no one knows the Father except the Son." But for this very reason, this verse has been called 'the Johannine Thunderbolt' because of its similarity to statements in John's Gospel, as contrasted with the way in which, elsewhere in the Synoptics,

Jesus generally directs our attention to his Father's Kingdom rather than to Himself.

The views of others in the Synoptics regarding the status of Jesus, seem to have varied, but they do not include the idea of his deity. At Mark (8:27), Jesus asks the disciples who do men think that he is. They reply that some think that he is John the Baptist, others Elijah, and others, one of the Prophets (no difficulty, apparently, about the resurrection of these figures).

When pressed for their own views, Peter tells Jesus that he is the Christ. But the Christ (Messiah) only means the anointed one of God, someone who was regarded as the human agent of God.

However, Paul (and presumably his converts) do appear to have believed that Jesus was almost God. In Philippians (2:6–11) (a Pauline letter considered to be genuine, and written in about 58 CE) Paul writes that Jesus, though he was in the form of God, did not count equality with God, a thing to be exploited, and he urges, "every tongue should confess that Jesus is Lord." (Philippians, 2:11). The Greek word kurios, here translated as 'Lord' does not necessarily imply divinity. It can mean simply 'master' or 'guide.' But when this is read in conjunction with v.6, some proximity to deity does seem to be affirmed. At Colossians (1:15–19), Paul (or one of his disciples, since it is not certain that Paul was the author of the letter), in somewhat more extravagant language, does connect Jesus with God and with creation: "He is the image of the invisible God, the first-born of all creation; for in him all things were created, through him and for him. He is, therefore, before all things, and in him all things hold together. For in him all the fullness of God was pleased to dwell." Since this letter was also written in about 58 CE, we must acknowledge that while it is very difficult to find the idea of Jesus as God within Jesus' own teaching, he was certainly seen by Paul and his mainly Gentile converts to be very close to deity not long after his death. This would seem to approximate to what was later to be known as the Arian view. The phrase 'the first-born of all creation' presages the Arian claim that 'there was a time when he was not.'

Continuing Monotheism

But Jesus' contemporaries had, in the main, considered him to be a prophet, while his disciples believed that he was also the Messiah (Christ). It is most unlikely, however, that they would have considered him to be divine, since this would have implied a breach with their strict monotheism. After his death, Jesus' followers certainly continued to behave as observant Jews. At Luke (24:53), we are told that after the Ascension the Eleven "were continually in the Temple, blessing God" and in Acts (2:46), Luke reports that the increasing number of Christians daily attended the Temple together. In Acts (6:7) it is even asserted that a great many of the priests in Jerusalem were obedient to the faith, and at 15:5 the Pharisees who had become believers argued that Gentile Christians needed to be circumcised and asked to keep the Mosaic Law. It is extremely unlikely that in such a strictly Jewish milieu, any idea of the deity of Jesus could have been entertained.

James, the brother of Jesus, was called 'the Just' because of his piety and strict observance of the Law. Despite the authority given to Peter (Matthew 16:18–19), it seems that James was the acknowledged head of the Church in Jerusalem, from soon after the death of Jesus (Acts 12:17), until his lynching in CE 62. James is also reported to have adjudicated at the Council of Jerusalem in CE 49 (Acts 15:19–20), and his decision was considered authoritative in the churches of Antioch, Syria and Cilicia (15:23). At this earliest stage in the history of the Church, the followers of Jesus were known as "belonging to the Way" (9:2). But they were still thought of as part of Judaism, revering Yahweh, the God of the Jews, the Law and the Temple, though 'the Way' was regarded as a sect (Greek haeresis) within Judaism (24:14), by virtue of its special attachment to Jesus.

This alienation of the Jewish Christians developed into hostility, when at the beginning of the siege of Jerusalem, they fled across the river Jordan to Pella, (the Greek Decapolis), though Eusebius' report of this flight has been doubted by S.G.F, Brandon and others. But the continued attendance of Jewish Christians at the synagogues threatened the insertion into the prayer known as the Eighteen Benedictions (90 CE) of an imprecation: "Let Nazarenes and heretics perish in a moment." Perhaps the final break with the orthodox synagogues came when, according to Justin Martyr (Apology 31), an individual known as BarKokhbar, who claimed to be the Jewish Messiah, and who had been acknowledged as such by Rabbi Aquiba, revolted against Rome. The Christians, naturally, could not support him.

The theological views of these early Palestinian Jewish Christians were not uniform, but Epiphanius divides them into two groups, the Nazarenes and the Ebionites. The latter were either named after one Ebion, or perhaps the title was derived from an Aramaic word meaning 'the poor' (cf. Paul's collection for 'the saints at Jerusalem', (1 Corinthians 16:1–3). Both groups believed in one God, the creator of the world, and they followed the Jewish way of life according to the Law. They observed both the Sabbath and circumcision. The Ebionites rejected the Virgin Birth, held Christ to be a mere man, and argued that Jesus had to merit his title, Christ, by fulfilling the Law. The Nazarenes probably accepted the Virgin Birth, but they denied Jesus' pre-existence as God, and called him the Son of God. According to Epiphanius, in many communities in Syria, Cyprus and Mesopotamia, the Ebionites had their own synagogues and elders. But they seem to have died out around the 4th century. Strict monotheism seems to have persisted as long as there were Jews of Palestinian origin who were also Christians. But by the time of their demise, the baton of Unitarian Christianity had been taken up by Gentiles.

Growing Diversity

As we have already seen, St Paul and his Gentile converts had in the early 50 CE ascribed to Jesus a status almost equal to deity. But when the full doctrinal consequences of this were appreciated, the conflict between inherited monotheism and the experience of 'something more than human' in Jesus resulted in a kaleidoscope of differing and confusing positions.

Against Gnosticism, with its myriads of intermediate beings between God and the world, the Monarchical Christians, influenced by the Jewish inheritance, insisted that there was one God only, the Maker and Ruler of the world.

But how was consciousness of the divinity of Christ, felt by many Christians, to be reconciled with this? One class of the Monarchians (the Rationalists) responded by treating Jesus' divinity as a power or status bestowed on him by God, either at his baptism or later. Two Christians, both known as Theodotus, were amongst the first who held this view. One was a leather-seller and the other a banker in Rome in the late 2nd century. The former is said by Tertullian to have regarded Christ as a mere man, though born of a virgin. They both laid stress on the humanity of Jesus and on the Synoptists' record of him, as opposed to the Johannine view of him as the divine Word or Logos of God. But they also believed that at his baptism he had been endowed with superhuman power. Artemon, a slightly later member of this Roman school, appealed to Scripture and the Apostles' preaching in support of his views. He claimed that all the Roman bishops down to Victor (who reigned 189–99CE) had been of this opinion, and that it was therefore an innovation to describe Christ as God. Needless to say, this claim was vigorously disputed!

The most famous champion of so-called Rationalist Monarchianism was Paul of Samosata of Syria, who in 260CE became Bishop of Antioch and Chancellor to Zenobia, Queen of Palmyra, and the ruler of Antioch at this time. Paul argued that Christ had been identified by the majority (i.e. the 'orthodox') with the personification of Divine Wisdom (as in Proverbs 8:22–31), and with the Word of God (Greek 'logos') as in the prologue to John's gospel. But stressing again the unity of God, he, also denied that these concepts implied separate persons. He insisted that they were attributes of God. The personality of Jesus, he said, was entirely human. But the divine power within him grew greater as he developed, enabling him finally to encompass divinity. Paul's life-style was questioned by some, and he was accused of excessive worldliness. But it is highly likely that his views influenced Arius, and their effect lived on until the 5th century through Theodore of Mopsuestia and Nestorius.

The Rise and Fall of Arianism

It is significant, that all of these early Gentile Christian thinkers granted Jesus super-human or supernatural powers, but denied that he was part of the one God. Their 'Unitarianism' therefore, was of a milder form than that of many thinkers in more recent times, who regarded Jesus as only a man, like a prophet, but also as one who, through his closeness to his Father, was able to reveal his Father's will. Indeed, Arius, perhaps the greatest of all heresiarchs, a presbyter of Alexandria, whose teaching first came into prominence about 317, called Christ God and Son of God, and offered him worship. But Arius was anxious to make Christianity more acceptable to those whose whole conception of God and culture was heathen. In this respect, he can be compared to Bishop J W Colenso (see above), the remarkable Victorian Churchman whose efforts to bring Christianity to the natives of South Africa led him to adopt a radical theology. Arius had also concluded that if Christ really was the Son of God, then the Father must have existed before him. The Son therefore, was not eternal. He must have been a created being. Hence, the famous Arian aphorism: "There was a time when the Son was not." (i.e., did not exist.) This teaching aroused the opposition of Arius' bishop, Alexander, and when Arius would not yield, he convened a synod which deposed Arius. Arius, however, had friends in ecclesiastical high places, and many bishops (and even the Emperor Constantine), urged Alexander to restore Arius. But such strong feelings had been aroused that Constantine summoned a Council of the Church, which met at Nicaea in Bithynia in CE 325, where 318 bishops assembled, but this was only one-sixth of the total body of bishops. The Council met amidst imperial splendour since Constantine was celebrating the twentieth year of his reign, and was anxious to consolidate his personal position. Many bishops supported Arius, but Constantine's adviser, Bishop Hosius of Cordova, was strongly against him. Thanks to the influence of the Emperor, advised by Hosius, the Nicaean Creed was finally adopted. Among other things, this affirmed that the Son was equal to the Father, of the same substance (Greek homoousios), 'very God from very God.'

Arius was banished and it was decreed that anyone baptised or ordained by Paul of Samosata had to be re-baptised or re-ordained. This implied that up to this point, they had not in fact been true Christians. The long shadow of that decision extends even until today!

However, Arius' claims to represent orthodoxy were not dead, and when Constantius became Emperor in 350 CE, he convened Church Councils in 353 and 355, specifically to condemn Athanasius, the inflexible opponent of Arius and an extreme Trinitarian, who, in 356 only escaped death by fleeing into the desert. What is more, at the Council of Smirmium in 357 CE, the bishops agreed upon another creed which suggested that the Son was not really God, declared the inferiority of the Son and other created things, and forbade the use of the terms 'one substance' or 'essence', on the ground that such expressions are not found in the Scriptures and reflect something which transcends human knowledge. But in spite of this, at the Council of Constantinople in 381 CE, the Nicaean Creed was again imposed as the standard of orthodoxy, and the equal Godhead of the Father and the Son has been proclaimed by the mainstream churches ever since.

But even this by no means spelt the end of Arianism. Many of the Goths converted in the 4th century by Ulfilla (c.311–383) were converted not to orthodoxy but to Arianism, and the Goths spread their Arianism to other Germanic tribes (Visigoths, Vandals, etc.). These tribes gradually overran the Roman Empire, which finally fell in 476 CE. But even the Arian conquerors were ultimately won over to Trinitarian orthodoxy.

The orthodox, being ipso facto the majority, were henceforth able to persecute minority Christian views as 'heresy' (Greek, haeresis—which means literally, and ironically, 'choice.') So anti-Trinitarian voices were finally silenced until the Reformation, when brave men like Michael Servetus, Francis David and the Socini in the 16th century, and John Biddle in the 17th, fearlessly proclaimed their Unitarian convictions. But that story is better-known.

Chapter 8
Free Christianity

Lest Free Christianity be lost in the shadows cast by its larger partner, Unitarianism, we intend to outline its distinctive nature, historical development and present importance.

Nature of Free Christianity

In this context 'Free' does not mean free in the sense of the freedom from state control which is possessed by all the nonconformist 'Free Churches'; it means Christianity unrestricted by a required acceptance of dogma or recital of creed. Free Christian chapels welcome all who wish to worship God and to learn about Jesus of Nazareth.

Those who accept this invitation may vary widely in their theological views. They may be Trinitarian or Unitarian or just uncertain about the status and mission of Jesus. For example, they may believe that his death took away the sins of the world, or was primarily a supreme example of self-sacrificial obedience to God's will. Free Christianity has been criticised on the ground that so broad an acceptance of different viewpoints leads to an ambiguous, nebulous kind of faith.

Vulnerability to this criticism has been inherited from English Presbyterianism; 'L' wrote in *The Christian Reformer* of 1842, that he had "found in connexion with the use of the word 'Presbyterian' a prevailing advocacy of a sort of generalised Christianity and an indifference to peculiar doctrines... for what is religion if it exist not in some distinct and determinate form? Is it possible that any serious Christian could enrol himself a member of a congregation where

Trinitarianism was preached one Sunday and Unitarianism the next, and where a succession of ministers filled the pulpit in turns, some of whom supported and others denounced, the doctrine of original sin, the vicarious sufferings of Christ, and election and reprobation?" (Vol. IX, p.771).

But the congregation does not usually hear a Trinitarian one Sunday and a Unitarian the next—the one resident minister when expounding any subject, be it original sin, the effect of the death of Jesus, or election, should explain both the majority and the minority Christian viewpoints in order to assist the hearer to formulate his private judgement on the various issues.

Twelve years later, *The Christian Reformer* contrasted the vigour of a sect with the weakness of non-sectarianism in reviewing a sermon preached by Rev. Charles Beard on 'The Unitarian Position'. "…We have no course open to us, in the assertion of what we believe to be Christian truth, but to continue to be a sect, although we may generally avoid the sectarian spirit." In following the worship commanded by revelation, we cannot avoid the way which other men choose to call "heresy". Mr Beard in his discourse strikes indirectly a heavy blow against the sickly non-sectarianism which has recently raised its feeble voice amongst us, and which if it were to lead captive the Unitarian body, would put back the cause of free enquiry and theological reform."

If we can identify this non-sectarianism as Free Christianity, we do not see that the cause of free enquiry is retarded. Free Christianity encourages the worshipper to pursue his own religious quest. If his quest leads him to a different Christian stance, that can be nurtured in his chapel; if it draws him to a non-Christian faith, then he will retain the goodwill of the chapel, but will probably find the form of worship at the citadel of his new faith more compatible. For Free Christians are not exclusive, but recognise that God has revealed himself through the prophets of many faiths, and, indeed, in many other ways. Thus, few of them would accept the authenticity of Jesus' claim at John 14:6 that nobody comes to the Father except by him.

In relation to this charge of 'sickly non-sectarianism', it has to be admitted that the widely divergent views within Free Christianity do demand from its members a tolerance over the content and language of the liturgy. The Unitarian Christian members have to tolerate the attribution to Jesus of divine and redemptive qualities in some hymns (especially Christmas carols), but the singing of the attributes does not predicate that the singer adopts the views of the writer—anymore than the public reader of a Pauline letter is identified with the views of Paul. There is no reason to treat the singing of a hymn as the recital of a creed. Reciprocally, the Trinitarian Christian members should not demur if the minister, in deference to Unitarians, generally omits Trinitarian doxologies ('in the name of the Father, Son and Holy Spirit') at the end of prayers and other liturgy, and addresses intercession to God the Father rather than to Jesus.

The variety of names—Mass, Eucharist, Holy Communion, Lord's Supper, Breaking of Bread—reflects the wide range of Christian views about what is happening at that service and indicates the need for sensitivity in its celebration in Free Christianity. Here also, however, the sympathetic attempt to serve the religious needs of all need not reduce the content of the service to a vapid lowest common denominator. The traditional invocation of the Holy Spirit upon the elements (bread and wine) can be broadened into a prayer that God will be especially present to the communicants so that their participation in the re-enactment of the Last Supper may bring spiritual grace in the way each of them desires. The minister can explain how Paul's statement at Corinthians (11: 23–24), that Jesus identified the broken bread with his body (broke and said) supports the minority view that Jesus was simply 'acting out' that he was to die for them, while Mark's statement at 14:22 describing bread as his body when giving it to the disciples (gave and said) supports the majority view that the bread is spiritual food. These divergent scriptural authorities justify the Unitarian in treating the service as a remembrance of Jesus' self-sacrifice in supreme obedience to what he believed to be his Father's will, and the Trinitarian additionally can view the consumption of the elements as bestowing special spiritual grace. To facilitate these different interpretations of what is happening, the words of distribution need to be as neutral or as versatile as possible, e.g. 'the broken bread of Jesus', 'the poured wine of Jesus'. We place in the Appendix a form of service which we have partly drafted for celebration of the last supper.

We think that a Free Christian congregation will have little difficulty in exercising the necessary tolerance on the above matters, since they are secondary to the unifying desire to worship God, and to follow his will as revealed by the prophets of Israel, and especially in the life and teaching of Jesus.

Notes on the History of Free Christianity

"Go nowhere among the Gentiles and enter no town of the Samaritans, but go rather to the lost sheep of the house of Israel." (Matthew 10: 5)

A concern for comprehension or inclusiveness is not readily perceived in Christianity's parent, the religion of Israel. In Isaiah 56, Gentiles are assured that all who have 'joined themselves to the Lord' will be brought to Mount Zion for "my house shall be called a house of prayer for all peoples". But this invitation is limited to Gentiles who 'keep the Sabbath… and hold fast my covenant', so it is, in effect, a welcome to Gentiles only if they will become Jews.

However, from the 2nd century BCE, Gentiles who worshipped the one God, Yahweh, and attended the synagogue and Temple but chose not to be circumcised and consequently observe the whole of the law, had a distinct identity within Judaism. They were attracted by the ethical principles and the monotheism of the Jews, and there are several references to them in the New Testament . They were known as 'God-fearers'.

Jesus wished to include everyone in the brotherhood of his followers. Although he defined his mission as being primarily to Israel (e.g. Matthew 10:5; Mark 7:27), he exorcized the Syrophoenician's daughter (Mark 7: 25-30) and healed the centurion's servant (Luke 7:1–10). Similarly inclusive was his attitude to those who wished to be associated with him. At Mark 9:38 he reproves his disciples who try to curb an independent healer who is healing in Jesus' name, and he is indignant when the disciples turn away mothers bringing their little children to him for blessings (Mark 10:13–16): he welcomes the blind man whom many had rebuffed (Mark 10:46–52).

It is Jesus' all-embracing attitude that Free Christians seek to continue by avoiding a name which separates one Christian from another, and by welcoming all who simply wish to learn about or follow the teaching of Jesus as inspired by the prophets of Israel. Attenders' views on doctrinal matters such as the Trinity, the atonement and the nature of the resurrection are considered of secondary importance, and in any case, matters of private judgement, not of public recital in a common creed.

The founder of Free Christianity in England is generally acknowledged to be Richard Baxter (1615–1691). Originally conformist to the Church of England, he was ordained by the Bishop of Worcester in 1638, and for 16 years was the parish minister at Kidderminster. Even at this early stage by a 'steady discouragement of party spirit', he acquired an extraordinary moral influence over his people. Briefly during the Civil War, he was a chaplain in the parliamentary army, but, although he praised the enlightened tolerance of Cromwell, he remained loyal to the national church.

At the restoration of the monarchy (Charles 11) and bishops in 1660 Baxter was acknowledged as leader of the Presbyterians. He was offered the Bishopric of Hereford, which he refused on grounds of conscience, and was made by Charles II a member of the Savoy Commission for reforming the Book of Common Prayer. Although he laboured indefatigably to achieve amendments to the Book which would permit Presbyterian clergy (and Independents who wished) to remain in their vicarages, his hopes of a comprehensive national church were dashed by the bishops who would agree few alterations to the Book as put forward by them. The intransigence of the bishops led to about 2,000 Presbyterian incumbents leaving their livings because they were unable in conscience to sign the 'assent and consent' to everything in that Book. It also provoked the personal persecution of Baxter for the next 25 years.

These Presbyterians might well have been called Anglican Puritans, for they were Puritans who wished to return within the national church to the purity of the early New Testament church, as opposed to those Puritans who wished to establish that purity in gathered congregations outside the Anglican church and were thus called 'Independents'. The Presbyterians, as their name suggests, desired to move towards church government by elders which they found in the New Testament, although they were willing to settle for a reformed system of bishops (episcopacy). However, they are the ancestors of the Free Christians, because under the influence of Baxter and others they came to place great value on the freedom of the individual to reach his own decision on religious matters. 'Parliamentary' Presbyterianism, in the sense of Scottish Presbyterianism, with its layered system of Church government which was accepted by Charles I in return for help from the Scottish Army in the Civil War, never gained a secure foothold in England.

Baxter was also a member of a group called the Reconcilers, and this description fits him admirably for he used all his influence to find some way of comprehension and compromise which would lead Presbyterians and Independents into the national church. "Look on all particular churches as members of the universal," he said in 1659, "And choose the best thou canst for thy ordinary communion… But deny not occasional communion with any (though accused by others), further than they may force thee to sin or that they separate from Christ." Ahead of his times, he even found hope for non-Christians, "I can never believe that a man may not be saved by that religion which doth but bring him to the true love of God and to a heavenly mind and life; nor that God will ever cast a soul into hell that truly loveth him." In his effort to avoid tests which would act as barriers to his Master's fold, he led a movement for the Reduction of Essentials or Fundamentals, and would require only acceptance of the Lord's prayer, the Apostles' Creed and the Ten Commandments for entry to the Church of Christ.

Baxter's Reduction of Essentials was the matrix from which developed the later Presbyterian promotion of free enquiry in religion. This facilitates the holding of many different views within the same congregation. Martineau contrasted in 1888 the habit of mind of Unitarian leaders, such as Lindsey and Priestley, who imported from their previous orthodox denominations the expectation that their new theology required a new creed. He wrote, "They did not observe that the very people they joined had insensibly passed through the whole distance between their old and their present theology, without any breach of the communion of worship or disturbance to the continuity of their history. There is no doubt some difficulty in resuming the name "English Presbyterianism" after having allowed it to fall into disuse. But every suggested alternative is attended, I think, with more serious difficulty." Nevertheless the alternative of 'Free Christian' was, in fact adopted to succeed 'Presbyterian', as the name for this Baxterian Christianity which seeks to embrace all who follow the teaching of Jesus but without restricting private judgement on doctrinal issues.

Although the clergy ejected in 1662 had mainly been of orthodox belief, and had declined to assent largely due to liturgical and disciplinary objections, once they were free to worship without persecution following the Toleration Act of 1689 (except in theory Catholics and anti-Trinitarians), they also felt freer to dissent over matters of doctrine. Although a Unitarian tendency in the form of Arianism first flourished in England amongst Anglicans at the beginning of the 18th century, many Presbyterian congregations had adopted definite Unitarian views by the middle of that century. Sometimes, this happened insensibly, but sometimes a confrontation was the watershed of change. For example, when at Bridport in 1742, the deacons noticed that the Rev. Thomas Collins "did not exalt the Saviour in his sermons as formerly", they asked him "do you believe that Jesus Christ was God, equal with the Father from all eternity?" At his negative reply, two hundred of the congregation withdrew. There thus arose a division of attitude between the Presbyterian congregations which preserved the comprehensive stance, seeking to serve all Christians whatever their doctrines, and the formerly Presbyterian congregations which had adopted a specific Unitarian Christian theology. Soon new chapels were founded, bearing from the outset the Unitarian name, beginning with Theophilus Lindsey's Essex Street Chapel in 1774.

In the first half of the 19th century, the Presbyterian congregations, many of which were now Unitarian, were in decline. In a back-handed compliment, 'L' wrote to *The Christian Reformer* in 1843, "I highly honour the English

Presbyterians to whom religion owes the greatest obligations... It has, however, had its day; and if it had not resulted in the profession of Unitarianism by a very great majority indeed of the Presbyterian congregations, the sect would probably, by this time, have been completely extinct; for where is English Presbyterianism except in the form of Unitarianism?" (volume X, p.236). Dr Bostock in a letter to *The Christian Reformer* in 1834 had earlier diagnosed the cause of the decline; he claimed that 40 years ago, Presbyterian societies 'were formed upon the principle of not admitting any restriction... on the freedom of enquiry in matters of religious belief; [they] were always urged to search the Scriptures and to read all kinds of books which might throw light upon them, yet there was comparatively little anxiety manifested respecting the conclusions which were formed... But an unfortunate change now took place. Causes... led to various polemical discussions. These produced their ordinary effect of exasperating the feelings of those engaged in them, and inducing them to magnify the importance of topics on which they had bestowed so much attention... The effect need scarcely be pointed out. The advocates for free enquiry now became the advocates for certain opinions; societies were formed not to discover the truth but to propagate those opinions... Hence, a body of men whose professed object was to promote free enquiry, virtually bound themselves to a set of opinions."

Yet, the comparative fortunes of Presbyterianism and Unitarianism probably ebbed and flowed, for the same 'L' had written to *The Christian Reformer* in the previous year bewailing the preference given in the Reformer's pages to the description 'Presbyterian' for churches which used to be styled 'Unitarian'. "I fear we are beginning to be ashamed of our 'Unitarianism'." He writes (volume. IX, p.770), "'Presbyterian' has now become the favourite word to designate those who are members of what used to be frequently styled in the by-gone time 'Unitarian congregations'." Probably the renewed regard for the Presbyterian style was motivated in part by the desire of congregations to retain chapels and endowments, which around this time were being claimed by Independents (Congregationalists) on the ground that the chapels were being used for non-Trinitarian worship in breach of the terms of the religious trusts upon which they were granted by the original donors. This fear of ouster from the chapels was removed on the passing of the Dissenters' Chapels Act in 1844.

The Presbyterians had suffered through having no national organisation; indeed, they would have considered themselves schismatic were it otherwise, for they believed they were exiled only temporally from the national church. However, in 1834, the first volume of *The Gospel Advocate* reported it had received copies of a 'proposed scheme' for establishing a Church on the Presbyterian model for Great Britain and Ireland, containing the following terms: "Every member of this Church professes his belief in the existence, attributes, providence and moral government of God; the Divine Mission, miracles and resurrection of Jesus Christ; and in the authority of the Holy Scriptures as the authentic records of Divine Revelation. But it is a fundamental principle of this Church to leave to every individual the unimpaired right of exercising his own private judgement in the interpretation of the Scriptures so that no creed of human invention, and relating to doctrines which are controverted among the professed followers of Jesus Christ, can be imposed by this Church..."

This scheme, devised by the Rev. James Yates of London did result in a Presbyterian Association, but it did not survive long.

The title 'Presbyterian' continued to lose favour in England, partly due to its ambiguity, but also to its confusion with Scottish Presbyterianism with whose fixity of doctrine and strict hierarchical government it had little affinity. A clearer title was found by some in 'Free Christian', and in an anniversary address reported in *The Christian Reformer* of 1863 the Pastor Rev John Robertson explained why the Free Christian Church at Halstead, Essex, chose that name six years earlier—"A few of us were Unitarians of a very decided character. There was no doubt about my preaching being Unitarian. Nothing seemed more natural, then, than to call ourselves a Unitarian society. But though my preaching was Unitarian, I had from the first inculcated the right and duty of free thought on matters pertaining to religion. I had also endeavoured to show, from the parables of and discourse of

Jesus that the Christianity of Christ is practical, and had condemned those who founded churches on principles narrower than those laid down by the Master. I could hardly, therefore, in justice, advocate the calling of our society by a name that would virtually exclude from membership all who did not hold my views of the Trinity. Moreover, many of the persons who had joined with us in worship here were not, at that time at least, prepared to call themselves Unitarian. They said, 'We like the liberty of thought you claim for every man, and we like still more the great doctrine you teach that salvation does not depend on the creed but the life; but as for the Trinity and other doctrines that from our infancy we have been taught to identify with Christianity, we hardly know what to say. On some of these questions our minds are in abeyance. This was a perfectly reasonable objection to a doctrinal name of any kind. It was clear that if we were to unite at all for any practical purpose, it must be under a name that would include varieties of opinion on theological questions. Hence, we called ourselves Free Christians... Our Presbyterian forefathers were most of them Calvinists, but they saw the evil of creeds and sectarian names; and when the law permitted them to build meeting houses for the worship of God, they left them with open trusts and unsectarian names... We are Free Christians then, because we would exclude no man from our communion on account of his opinions, and our bond of union is practical rather than speculative."

Not all Free Christian churches sprang from the Presbyterian tradition; some were established by former Congregational or Baptist ministers. On 11th July 1853, Rev. William Forster, who had left a prosperous Congregational Chapel, issued to the local inhabitants a leaflet seeking support for the 'Free Christian Church of Kentish and Camden Towns'. He wrote, "it is impossible to over-estimate the evil which has been done to the Christianity of Christ by the curb put upon the fullest exercise of private judgement... impressed with these lamentable evils, some of your neighbours have formed themselves into a Free Christian church, in which these abuses will have no place. We regard the Scriptures as the only rule of faith. We insist upon the duty of all men to inquire into religion for themselves. We maintain that each individual is responsible to God only for the conclusion to which he may arrive... We expect freedom of utterance in the Pulpit, and we claim freedom of investigation in the Pew."

But the Presbyterian/Unitarian chapels were the most affected. Also in 1853, Rev. Franklin Howorth, after 22 years, resigned his office at Bury Unitarians, despite earnest entreaties, and opened a place of worship in Bury for 'free and unsectarian Christian worship'. The Reformer's editor was stung by such departures to comment that year, "We have been a little jealous of some such avowed movements when they have seemed to cast an undeserved and most unhandsome slur upon the freedom of those very Churches whose principles and spirit they can only imitate. No Unitarian, minister or layman, need leave his present associates in search of liberty at any rate."

It will have become evident from the above historical sidelights that the main distinction between Unitarian Christianity (which was the original form of Unitarianism) and Free Christianity, both of which developed in large part from Presbyterianism, is that the former is sectarian, proclaiming its anti-Trinitarian belief and the views flowing from that, whereas Free Christianity, also includes Trinitarians and Christians of other or indeterminate belief because it seeks to serve all who wish to follow Jesus, whatever their doctrines.

A separate phenomenon, outside the above development, was the founding about this time of several churches of 'Freethinking Christians', of which a prominent example was the Church of God meeting at St John's Square, London. 'A Member' wrote to The Christian Reformer in 1842 (volume IX, pp 482–483) stating that its fundamental principles were the strict unity of God, reasonable service to the ascertained will of the One True God, and distinct union for that sacred purpose of 'The Church of God'. Its affinity to Free Christianity was clear from the affirmation that, "what is true can only be discerned by each person freely using his own private judgement, thinking and searching for himself to know the truth." No churches so denominated are thought to have survived.

The description, 'Free Christian' superseded English Presbyterianism and was given national prominence in the formation of 'The Free Christian Union' by James Martineau and others in 1866. Its formation was provoked by the attempts to have the term 'Unitarian Christianity' clearly defined at the meeting of the British and Foreign Unitarian Association (B&FUA) in 1865. These attempts were construed by some as intending to impose a virtual creed, and they summoned a meeting 'to consider the means of forming a closer union among liberal Christian Churches and persons for the promotion and application of religion in life, apart from doctrinal limitations in thought'. In response to an appeal to act as its leader in this venture, Martineau replied, "In regard to external relations, we stand at the very crisis of the world most favourable to the action of an undogmatic Church, a church unconditionally devoted to the pure Christian pieties and charities... The Church is the Society of those who seek harmony with God; and all who agree on the terms of that harmony, so as to seek it in the same way, belong to the same Church... whom accordingly would I admit to fellowship? All who seek harmony with God and are content with these terms. Whom would I exclude? Absolutely none; leaving the door forever open and letting all exclusion be self-exclusion." The Free Christian Union was formed and its meetings were attended by Anglican, Independent and Baptist clergy, in addition to Presbyterians, but there was a reluctance to work for the cause and even a contemplated volume of essays had to be abandoned. In 1870, Martineau himself proposed the dissolution of the Union, a sad end to his "earnest attempt to lift religion out of its sectarian ruts and make it wide and free as the kingdom of God".

Organisation of Free Christianity

In 1881, the B&FUA invited 'the ministers, members and friends of all Unitarian, Liberal Christian, Free Christian, Presbyterian and other Non-subscribing or Kindred Congregations' to a conference in April 1882 at Liverpool "in the hope that... it will assemble the ministers and members of our congregations on the broad platform of religion and morality". These conferences were held nearly every three years until 1926, and became a bastion of the anti-dogmatic

Presbyterian/Free Christian tradition; it was popularly known as 'The National Conference of Free Christian Churches'.

Martineau was encouraged to propose this conference as a national organisation of English Presbyterian congregations so that the stronger would contribute towards the financial support of the weaker, and the national minimum stipend thus secured would only be available to ministers who had an Arts degree and University theological training in addition to evidence of character. The name for the diverse categories named in the conference title would be subsumed into 'English Presbyterian', for 'Unitarian' was the expression of a personal belief. "If anyone, being a Unitarian, shrinks on fitting occasion, from plainly calling himself so, he is a sneak and a coward. If, being of our catholic communion, he calls his chapel or its congregation Unitarian, he is a traitor to his spiritual ancestry, and a deserter to the camp of its persecutors." But his practical proposals were too complicated, and his proposals foundered.

The National Conference of Free Christians lived on, however, and at the Conference of 1926, Mrs Sydney Martineau, a relative of James, proposed its amalgamation with the B&FUA. This alliance of the comprehensive Free Christians with the doctrinal Unitarian Christians was completed in 1928, but became uncomfortable in later years when the Unitarian name was claimed by non-Christians and humanists; today some Unitarians even consider Unitarianism to be an independent religion, separate and distinct from Christianity.

Conclusion

Many Unitarian Christians believe that the description 'Unitarian Christian' contains within it the comprehensive spirit of Free Christianity. But while this may be appreciated by 'insiders', the outside world, reading the words 'Unitarian Christian', can only understand thereby a kind of Christianity which is doctrinally restricted by the adjective 'Unitarian'. It is, therefore, important that not only the spirit but the name of Free Christianity is reserved both in the titles of chapels and in the name of the General Assembly; otherwise the breath of its peaceable life may be squeezed out by denominational forces which are constitutionally more powerful and temperamentally more assertive.

Yet so far, the descendants of the Free Christian element in that 1926 merger have managed to maintain the Presbyterian tolerance and warm inclusivity which they inherited. We can be sanguine about the future also, for what sentiment can be closer to the spirit of the Master than the Free Christian declaration of Dr John Taylor (1694–1761) at the opening of the Presbyterian Octagon Chapel at Norwich, "We are Christian and only Christians... we disown all connection, except that of love and goodwill, with any sect or party whatever... so that we may exercise the public duties of religion upon the most catholic and charitable foundation."

Appendix

(Readings, hymns and a homily may be inserted as required.)

Preparation. Minister —The Lord be with you. All —And with thy spirit.

The Lord's Prayer (unless prayed previously). All —Our Father, who art in heaven, hallowed be thy name. Thy kingdom come . Thy will be done on earth as it is in heaven. Give us this day our daily bread. And forgive us our trespasses, as we forgive those who trespass against us. And lead us not into temptation, but deliver us from the Evil One: for thine is the kingdom, the power and the glory, for ever and ever. Amen.

The Collect for Purity. All—Almighty God, unto whom all hearts be open, all desires known, and from whom no secrets are hid; cleanse the thoughts of our hearts by the inspiration of thy Holy Spirit; that we may perfectly love thee and worthily magnify thy holy Name; through Jesus Christ, our Lord. Amen.

The Summary of the Law. Minister—Jesus said: Hear, O Israel the Lord our God is one Lord; and thou shalt love the Lord thy God with all thy heart, and with all thy soul, and with all thy mind, and with all thy strength. This is the first commandment. And the second is like, namely this: Thou shalt love thy neighbour as thyself. There is none other commandment greater than these. On these two commandments hang all the law and the prophets. All—Lord, have mercy upon us , and write all these thy laws in our hearts, we beseech thee.

Introduction. Minister—Friends, in our service of Holy Communion we seek to draw near to our heavenly Father just as did the Israelites in the Temple who ate their communion sacrifices together, but left a place at the table for Him. So we would also keep a place at our table and in our hearts for Jesus, as we remember his last Supper. For we all seek to follow his command to eat the bread and to drink the wine in remembrance of him, and we pray that through our participation in that remembrance and in the bread and wine, we may receive grace to do our Father's will so that He may reign in our hearts and we may rest in his Kingdom.

Confession. Minister—Jesus said, "Suffer the little children to come unto me", and since our God is a Father of mercy like the father of the Prodigal Son, we can be assured that if we sincerely repent of our sins and intend to try to improve, then our prayers and our presence at His table will be welcomed by Him. Let us pray:
All—Father, you know that since we last confessed our sins we have not loved you with all our heart nor our neighbour as ourselves; we may have neglected our devotions to you—we may have wasted opportunities to do good—we may have done things which were not good—you, Father,, know our hearts. We are genuinely sorry for these our sins, and sincerely repent of them. We pray that our wills may be so strengthened by thy grace to resist temptation that we may serve you in the future in newness of life to the glory of your Name. Minister—May our heavenly Father who forgives all who sincerely repent, have mercy upon us, pardon and deliver us from our sins, strengthen us in all temptations, and keep us in his Kingdom; through Jesus Christ, our Lord. Amen.

General Intercessions. (unless prayed previously)

Words of Grace. Minister—Hear how our heavenly Father feeds us:
Then the Lord said to Moses, "Behold, I will rain bread from heaven for you; and the people shall go out and gather a day's portion every day, that I may prove them, whether they will walk in my law or not. I have heard the murmurings of the people of Israel; say to them, 'At twilight you shall eat meat

and in the morning you shall be filled with bread; then you shall know that I am the Lord your God.' (Exodus 16:4 and 12)

Jesus said to them, "I am the bread of life; he who comes to me shall not hunger, and he who believes in me shall never thirst." (John 6:35) Jesus also said, "Behold, I stand at the door and knock; if anyone hears my voice and opens the door, I will come in to him and eat with him and he with me." (Revelation 3:20.)

<u>The Supper</u>. Minister—Let us lift up our hearts. All—We lift them to the Lord.

Minister—Father, we ask you to bless this bread and this wine so that our reception of them may bring to us, each in our own way, such fellowship with you and with the spirit of your Son as may strengthen us to cleave to your Kingdom, and to encourage others towards it. Amen.

Minister—We break this bread to share in the body of Christ. Although we are many, we are one body because we all share the one bread.

Minister—An account of the Last Supper taken from the reports of Paul, Mark and Luke:

On the night when he was betrayed, Jesus said to his disciples, "I had earnestly desired to eat this passover with you before I suffer; for I tell you, I shall not eat it until it is fulfilled in the Kingdom of God." And he took bread, recited the blessing, broke the bread and said, "This is my body which is broken for you." He then gave the bread to them. He said, "Do this in remembrance of me." And he took the cup, recited the blessing, and said, "This is my blood which is poured out for many. My blood will solemnise the new covenant. Take this and divide it among yourselves; for I tell you that from now on I shall not drink of the fruit of the vine until the Kingdom of God comes." He then gave the cup to them. He said, "Do this, as often as you drink it, in remembrance of me."

Minister—Let us take and eat this bread in remembrance that Jesus died for us, and let us feed on him in our hearts by faith with thanksgiving. (The broken bread of Jesus.)

Let us drink this wine as a foretaste of the Messianic Banquet, that symbol of the heavenly Kingdom which, as Jesus taught, may reign in our hearts here and now. (The poured wine of the Kingdom.)

All—Under the veil of earthly things we now have communion with Jesus Christ; but with unveiled faces we shall soon behold him and, rejoicing in his glory, be made like him; and by him all his disciples will be presented before the presence of his Father's glory with exceeding joy. Father, we thank you for the fellowship with you and with the spirit of your Son and with each other which we have enjoyed this day through the remembrance of, and participation in, the Last Supper, and we rejoice to sing, like the angels on that first Christmas night:
Glory be to God on high and, on earth, peace, goodwill towards men. We praise thee, we bless thee, we give thee thanks, 0 Father everlasting, for all thy love to us in Jesus Christ, thy Son.

Conclusion. All—0 Lord, our heavenly Father, we offer you our souls and bodies to be a living sacrifice to you. Send us out in the power of the Spirit, to live and work to thy praise and glory. Amen.

* * * * *

Minister—May the peace of God, which passeth all understanding, and which the world can neither give nor take away, be with us now, and abide in our hearts for ever. Amen. Go in peace to love and serve the Lord.
All—In the name of Jesus Christ. Amen.

About the Author

Roger Booth is a retired solicitor who also taught law at the University of Buckingham. His degrees in theology are from King's College, London and his degree in law is from Leeds University. He was formerly minister at the Chapel in the Garden, Bridport, Dorset, England.

Other books by the author:
Jesus and the Laws of Purity, Sheffield Academic Press, 1987
Contrasts—Gospel Evidence and Christian Beliefs, Paget Press, 1990
The Bedrock Gospel: Sifting the Sources, Paget Press, 2001